AF264376

Greek Mythology for Beginners

The Myths of Ancient Greece Simplified for People Who Slept Through History Class

Free Bonus from Captivating History (Available for a Limited time)

Hi History Lovers!

Now you have a chance to join our exclusive history list so you can get your first history ebook for free as well as discounts and a potential to get more history books for free!

Simply visit the link below to join.

Or, Scan the QR code!

captivatinghistory.com/ebook

Also, make sure to follow us on Facebook, X, and YouTube by searching for Captivating History.

Table of Contents

Introduction
Why Should You Care About a Bunch of Dead Gods?

Let's start with a confession: Greek mythology is everywhere, and you probably didn't even notice.

That Nike swoosh on your shoes? Named after the Greek goddess of victory. The planet Mars orbiting in space? That's named after Ares, the god of war (known as Mars in Roman mythology). When someone talks about your "Achilles heel," they're referencing a legendary Greek warrior whose name became synonymous with a fatal weakness. When your friend is being narcissistic, they're channeling a guy who fell in love with his own reflection and died staring at it. Even the word "mythology" comes from Greek; *mythos* means "story," and *logos* means "study."

These aren't just dusty tales from three thousand years ago. They're the blueprint for how we tell stories today. Superhero movies, fantasy novels, and epic video games borrow from Greek myths. The patterns we see in modern storytelling—the hero who overcomes obstacles, the tragic character brought down by their own choices, the epic quest for glory— come from ancient Greece. Love triangles, family drama, and revenge plots were all perfected by people who lived before the invention of the printing press.

But Greek mythology isn't just about entertainment. These stories were how ancient Greeks explained their world. Why does winter happen?

Because a goddess is sad. Why do we suffer? Because a curious woman opened a jar she shouldn't have. Why do bad things happen to good people? Because the gods are petty and bored. The myths provided answers to questions that science couldn't touch yet.

They also reveal what the Greeks valued and feared. Hubris—excessive pride—was the ultimate sin. Hospitality to strangers was sacred. Revenge was expected. Glory in battle meant immortality through memory. These were moral lessons, religious texts, and historical records all rolled into one.

The Stage: Mountains, Islands, and Why Geography Matters

Greece isn't a flat country. It's a collection of rocky mountains, scattered islands, and isolated valleys separated by the sea. In ancient times, this geography gave rise to hundreds of independent city-states that rarely agreed on anything. Athens and Sparta might as well have been different countries.

This fractured landscape shaped the myths. Each city-state had its own patron god, its own local heroes, and its own version of events. Athens claimed Athena. Thebes honored Dionysus. Delphi belonged to Apollo.

The sea was central to Greek life. The Greeks were traders, sailors, and warriors who spent months at sea. So naturally, their myths are full of sea monsters, angry ocean gods, and sailors blown off course. Poseidon, god of the sea, was just as important as Zeus.

The mountains isolated communities but also inspired awe. The Greeks believed their gods lived on Mount Olympus, the highest peak they knew. It made sense. If you were a god, wouldn't you want the best view?

The Disclaimer: Multiple Versions and How to Read Myths

Here's something they probably didn't tell you in school: there's no single "correct" version of Greek mythology. The stories were passed down orally for centuries before anyone wrote them down. Different poets, playwrights, and historians recorded different versions. Homer's version might contradict Hesiod's. A vase painting might tell the story differently than a temple carving.

For example, some myths say Aphrodite was born from sea foam after Uranus's castrated genitals were thrown into the ocean. Other versions say she's the daughter of Zeus and a Titaness. Both versions existed at the same time. The Greeks didn't see this as a problem. Myths were flexible.

We'll be drawing primarily from the earliest sources, namely Homer's *Iliad* and *Odyssey*, Hesiod's *Theogony* and *Works and Days*, and various Greek tragedies and classical texts. When there are major differences among versions, I'll point them out. But don't expect neat, consistent timelines. Greek mythology is messy, contradictory, and wonderfully human.

Another important note is that these myths weren't written as literal history. The Greeks themselves debated whether the gods were real or metaphorical. By the time of philosophers such as Plato and Aristotle, many educated Greeks treated myths as allegories rather than as facts. The stories evolved over a thousand years, absorbing influences from Egypt, Mesopotamia, and other cultures the Greeks encountered.

We're going to explore these myths the way the Greeks themselves experienced them—as living, breathing stories that changed depending on who was telling them and why. We won't sanitize them. Greek myths are violent, sexual, and morally complicated. The gods are jealous, petty, and vengeful. Heroes commit terrible acts. There are no perfect characters.

But that's precisely why these stories have survived for millennia. They're not about perfect people or tidy morals. They're about flawed beings trying to navigate a world they don't fully control, a world where even gods make mistakes.

Does that sound familiar? That's because we're still living in it.

So buckle up. We're about to meet the most dysfunctional family in literary history, witness wars that last decades, and discover why you should never, ever trust a Greek god bearing gifts. These stories shaped Western civilization. They influenced our art, literature, psychology, and language.

And it all started with Chaos.

Chapter 1: In the Beginning... There was a Mess

Before there were gods, before there were humans, before there was anything recognizable as a world, there was Chaos.

Not chaos in the way we use the word today—not noise, disorder, or your teenager's bedroom. This was Chaos with a capital C. It was the primordial void. Pure nothingness. Or maybe pure everything so jumbled together that it hadn't separated into distinct things yet. The ancient Greeks weren't entirely clear on this point, and honestly, how could they be? Try describing absolute nothingness. It's impossible.

But from this Chaos, the first beings emerged. These were not the Greek gods we know. They were something older and stranger. These were the primordial deities—cosmic forces that shaped reality itself.

Chaos and the First Beings: From the Void to Gaia and Uranus

The poet Hesiod, writing around 700 BCE, gives us the earliest complete account of creation in his *Theogony*. According to Hesiod, the first thing to emerge from Chaos was Gaia, the Earth. Not a goddess who ruled over Earth. She was Earth. She was every mountain, every valley, and every stone. Gaia was the physical world itself, conscious and alive.

Think about what this means. When you walk on the ground, you're walking on a goddess. When a farmer plows a field, he's plowing her body. The Greeks saw the world as alive and aware. This wasn't exactly pantheism—it was something stranger. The Earth could think, feel, plan, and act.

Next came Tartarus, the deepest pit of the underworld, a place so far below the Earth that an anvil dropped from the surface would fall for nine days before hitting the bottom. Tartarus wasn't just a location. Like Gaia, he was a being. He was dark, vast, and terrifying. He represented the absolute lowest point of existence, the cosmic basement where the worst offenders would eventually be imprisoned.

Then Eros appeared. This was not the cute baby with arrows from Valentine's Day cards. This was primordial Eros, the fundamental force of attraction that would drive all creation. Without Eros, nothing would come together. There would be no unions, no offspring, or no new beings. Eros was the cosmic glue that held everything together; it represented whatever force made things desire to join and create. Some later philosophers, particularly Plato, would develop complex theories about this primordial love, but Hesiod keeps it simple. Eros was there from near the beginning, and Eros made everything else possible.

Finally, Nyx (Night) and Erebus (Darkness) emerged. These two represented the absence of light, but they were also incredibly powerful beings who would give birth to many important concepts. From their union came Aether (Upper Air) and Hemera (Day). Night also produced, on her own, a whole brood of abstract concepts made flesh: Moros (Doom), Thanatos (Death), Hypnos (Sleep), the Oneiroi (Dreams), Momus (Blame), Nemesis (Retribution), and the three Fates—Clotho, Lachesis, and Atropos—who would spin, measure, and cut the thread of every mortal life.

The fact that Night gave birth to Death tells you something important about Greek cosmology. Death wasn't a punishment from the gods. It was baked into the universe from the very beginning. It was as fundamental as darkness itself.

Now here's where it gets weird. Gaia, the Earth, decided she needed a partner. So she created one by herself. She gave birth to Uranus, the Sky, who became both her son and her husband. Yes, you read that right. The Greeks were not squeamish about these things. In the primordial age, the usual rules didn't apply. These weren't people. They were cosmic forces in the shape of beings.

Uranus spread himself over Gaia like a dome, creating the boundary between Earth and heaven. Every time it rained, that was Uranus fertilizing Gaia. Every storm was their passion. The ancient world didn't separate sex from natural processes. They were the same thing.

Together, Gaia and Uranus began producing children. Lots of them. And this is where the world as the Greeks knew it really began to take shape.

First came the Titans, twelve gigantic beings who ruled the cosmos before the Olympian gods. The eldest was Oceanus, who took the form of a great river encircling the entire world. Others included Hyperion and Theia (who would produce the Sun, Moon, and Dawn), Iapetus (who would father Prometheus and Atlas), Themis (divine law and order), and Mnemosyne (memory itself).

The youngest was Cronus, the most ambitious of the Titans. He would become king of the gods through violence—and he would lose that throne the same way. His sister-wife Rhea embodied fertility and motherhood. She was destined to suffer watching her children be devoured one by one.

But the Titans weren't the only children. Gaia and Uranus also produced the Cyclopes, three massive beings with a single eye in the center of their foreheads. Their names were Brontes (Thunder), Steropes (Lightning), and Arges (Brightness). In Hesiod's account, they are simply powerful and one-eyed. But as the stories evolved through later writers like Apollodorus, these Cyclopes became master craftsmen who could forge weapons with supernatural properties. They would eventually create Zeus's thunderbolts, Poseidon's trident, and Hades's helmet of invisibility. These weren't the monster Cyclopes who would later terrorize sailors in Homer's *Odyssey*; those were a different generation entirely.

Then came the Hecatoncheires, whose name literally means "hundred-handed ones." These three brothers—Cottus, Briareus, and Gyges—each had fifty heads and one hundred arms. Imagine the nightmare of that family reunion! They represented overwhelming force, the kind of power that couldn't be reasoned with or stopped, only contained.

Uranus looked at these last six children—the three Cyclopes and three Hecatoncheires—and was horrified. They were too strange, too monstrous, and too powerful. Perhaps he feared them. Perhaps he simply found them disgusting. Either way, he made a decision that would doom him.

He shoved them back inside Gaia.

And this was not in a metaphorical sense. He literally forced these enormous, many-headed, many-handed beings back into the Earth, imprisoning them in her depths. Gaia was in agony. Her own children were trapped inside her, causing her constant pain. She could feel them moving in the darkness below. But Uranus didn't care. He kept coming to her night after night, covering her completely so nothing could escape, perpetuating her suffering.

This was the original sin of the Greek cosmos. Not disobedience like in the Garden of Eden. Not pride like the Tower of Babel. Cruelty. A father's cruelty toward his own children. And a husband's indifference to his wife's pain.

Gaia would not forget. And she would have her revenge.

The Titans' Reign: The Rise of Cronus and the Original "Problematic Father" Trope

Gaia had reached her limit. Her husband-son Uranus had imprisoned her youngest children, and she was suffering. So, she did what any reasonable primordial Earth goddess would do. She plotted revenge.

She created a massive sickle from flint or adamantine; the sources disagree on the material, but they agree it was wickedly sharp. This was a harvesting tool, the kind used to cut wheat. The symbolism was clear: Uranus was about to be harvested.

Gaia approached her Titan children with a proposal. Someone needed to castrate Uranus. But the Titans were terrified. Uranus was the sky itself. He was all-powerful and all-seeing. How do you ambush someone who is everywhere? They refused. They loved their mother, but this was suicide.

But then, the youngest Titan, Cronus, stepped forward. He was ambitious, ruthless, and willing to do what others wouldn't. Some sources suggest he was motivated by genuine rage at his father's crimes. Others imply he simply saw an opportunity for power. Both were probably true.

Cronus agreed to his mother's plan. That night, when Uranus came down to lie with Gaia as he did every evening, Cronus was waiting. Gaia had hidden him in a secret spot—some say in her own body, others say behind an outcropping of rock. Cronus held the sickle and waited in the darkness.

When Uranus spread himself over Gaia, completely vulnerable in his passion, Cronus struck. He castrated his father with one brutal, decisive swing.

The blood from Uranus's wound fell to Earth in heavy drops. This wasn't ordinary blood; it was the creative essence of the sky itself. Where it landed, new beings sprang up. The Furies emerged—three sisters named Alecto, Megaera, and Tisiphone. They were vengeful spirits who punished crimes, especially crimes within families. The fact that they were born from an act of familial violence was fitting. They would haunt murderers and oath-breakers for all eternity.

The blood also created the Giants, a race of huge warriors who would later make war on the Olympian gods, and the Meliae, nymphs of the ash trees, who would nurse the infant Zeus.

Even Uranus's severed genitals had creative power. Cronus took them and threw them into the sea. They drifted on the waves, and around them foam gathered, white and pure. From this sea foam, the goddess Aphrodite would eventually be born, already fully grown and impossibly beautiful. Yes, the goddess of love and sex was born from an act of brutal violence. The Greeks understood that passion and violence were closer than we like to admit.

The famous Birth of Venus by Sandro Botticelli.[1]

Uranus, wounded and humiliated, retreated to the upper sky. He cursed Cronus with a prophecy: you too will be overthrown by your own children, just as you have overthrown me. Then he withdrew from the world, becoming the distant, unreachable heaven. He remained as the physical sky, but he would never again descend to Earth or interact with his children. He became passive and indifferent, merely the backdrop against which everything else happened.

With Uranus gone, Cronus took power. He freed his Titan siblings from their assigned positions and claimed kingship over the cosmos. The age of the Titans had begun.

Cronus took his sister Rhea as his wife. This wasn't unusual for the gods. The Titans kept to themselves, so they married each other. Together, Cronus and Rhea ruled from Mount Othrys, the Titans' stronghold.

Oddly enough, while Cronus was a nightmare to his own family, a different tradition found in Hesiod's other work, *Works and Days*, describes his reign as a golden age for humanity. This was supposedly a time of prosperity and peace for early humans. The earth gave food without labor. Men lived simply, like gods, without sorrow or toil. There was no war, no disease, and no old age. When death came, it was like falling asleep. Whether this contradictory portrait of Cronus reflects different traditions or simply the fact that tyrants can preside over prosperity, we don't know.

What we do know is that Cronus himself was not at peace. His father's curse haunted him. The prophecy repeated in his mind. One of his children would overthrow him, just as he had overthrown Uranus. The fear ate at him. He trusted no one and suspected everything. Paranoia became his constant companion.

So when Rhea gave birth to their first child—a daughter named Hestia—Cronus made a terrible decision. He took the baby and swallowed her whole.

He did not kill her. The gods were immortal and couldn't die. But she was trapped. Hestia remained conscious in her father's stomach, growing in the darkness, aware but helpless.

Rhea was devastated. But what could she do? Cronus was king of the universe. He had the support of most of the Titans. His word was law. When their second child was born—another daughter, Demeter—Cronus swallowed her too. Hera, Hades, and Poseidon followed. They were all swallowed.

Saturn, Jupiter's father, devours one of his sons *by Peter Paul Rubens.*[2]

Cronus had become exactly what he destroyed. He had struck down his father for his cruelty to children, and now he was committing the same crime. The cycle of violence had continued. Power doesn't redeem. It corrupts. The victim becomes the abuser. The rebel becomes the tyrant.

Rhea had suffered enough. When she became pregnant for the sixth time, she went to her parents, Gaia and the weakened Uranus, for help. Gaia, who had orchestrated the downfall of Uranus, now plotted the downfall of Cronus. The cycle would turn again.

Together, the two devised a plan.

The War of the Generations: The Titanomachy

When Rhea's sixth child was born—a son—she didn't bring him to Cronus. Instead, she took a large stone, wrapped it in swaddling clothes, and presented it to her husband.

Cronus was apparently not the brightest Titan, as he swallowed the stone without even looking. Perhaps he was too paranoid to think clearly. Perhaps he simply didn't care enough to check. Either way, he never noticed the deception.

The real baby, named Zeus, was spirited away to the island of Crete. There, in a cave on Mount Ida (or Mount Dicte, depending on which version you read), he was raised in secret. The nymphs Adrasteia and Ida fed him honey. The goat Amalthea nursed him with her milk. The warriors called the Curetes danced and clashed their shields whenever the baby cried, drowning out the sound so Cronus wouldn't hear and come looking.

Zeus grew up far from his father's realm, knowing he was destined for something greater. And as he grew, so did his anger at what had been done to his siblings.

When Zeus reached adulthood, he returned to challenge Cronus. But he needed a plan. He couldn't just walk up to the king of the Titans and demand a fight. He needed some kind of an advantage.

With Gaia's help, he disguised himself as a cupbearer in Cronus's court. Some versions say the goddess Metis (Wisdom) helped him by preparing a special potion. Zeus approached his father and offered him a drink—a mixture of wine, honey, and mustard that would make him vomit.

Cronus, not recognizing his son, drank it down. The effect was immediate and violent. He began to vomit uncontrollably.

First came the rock that Cronus had thought was Zeus. It flew from his mouth and landed on the earth. Later, this stone would be set up at Delphi as a monument, proof that even the mightiest could be deceived.

Then, one by one, Zeus's siblings emerged. Poseidon came first since he'd been swallowed last. Hestia was the last to be freed. They came out fully grown and ready for war.

The six siblings immediately formed an alliance. Zeus was the natural leader; he was the one who'd freed them, after all. However, they were equals in power. They had a score to settle with their father and with the Titan regime that had allowed such cruelty.

Zeus's next move was strategic. He descended to Tartarus, the deepest pit of the underworld, and freed the Cyclopes and Hecatoncheires—those monstrous children Uranus had imprisoned ages ago. He promised them freedom and vengeance if they would fight for him.

They agreed. They had been imprisoned for eons, first by Uranus, then by Cronus. They wanted revenge.

In gratitude for their freedom, the Cyclopes forged weapons of incredible power. For Zeus, they made the thunderbolt, a weapon that could destroy anything. This concentrated blast of lightning could crack mountains and kill immortals. For Poseidon, they forged the trident—a three-pronged spear that could summon earthquakes, split stone, and control the seas. For Hades, they created a helmet of invisibility (known as the Helm of Darkness) that would make the wearer impossible to see, hear, or detect.

With these weapons, Zeus and his siblings declared war on Cronus and the Titans.

The Titanomachy—the war between Titans and Olympians—lasted ten years. These years of constant, brutal warfare nearly destroyed the cosmos.

The armies assembled. On one side stood the Titans, led by Cronus, with most of his brothers supporting him. Atlas, the son of Iapetus, became Cronus's greatest general. Menoetius, another son of Iapetus, fought for the Titans with savage fury. Most of the older generation rallied to Cronus's banner, seeing the younger gods as upstarts who needed to be put down.

On the other side stood Zeus and his five siblings, supported by the Cyclopes and Hecatoncheires. They also had some surprising allies. Themis, the Titaness of divine law, sided with Zeus. She could see that the old order was unjust and needed to fall. Oceanus, the great river Titan, remained neutral, refusing to fight for either side. Most importantly, Prometheus and his brother Epimetheus, sons of the Titan Iapetus, joined Zeus's cause. Prometheus could see the future, and he knew which side would win.

The gods chose Mount Olympus as their fortress, the highest peak in Greece. The Titans held Mount Othrys to the south. The Earth became a battlefield.

Zeus hurled thunderbolts that scorched the Earth and split the sky. Mountains caught fire. Poseidon struck the ground with his trident, causing earthquakes that reshaped coastlines and swallowed entire valleys. The sea boiled and surged. Tidal waves crashed across the land.

The Hecatoncheires were devastating. Each one could grab a hundred boulders at once and hurl them like missiles. They were living siege weapons, unstoppable engines of destruction. Ancient sources say they threw three hundred rocks at once, creating barrages that darkened the sky.

Hades wore his helmet of invisibility and crept into the Titans' camps, spreading fear and confusion. He would appear without warning, strike, and then vanish. The Titans never knew where he'd come from or where he'd gone.

The Titans fought back with equal fury. Atlas was nearly invincible in combat. Menoetius fought with such rage that even the Olympians feared him. The battle raged for a decade, neither side able to gain a decisive advantage.

Until Zeus unleashed the full power of his alliance.

He brought the Hecatoncheires to the front lines and told them to hold nothing back. The three brothers unleashed a storm of stone that overwhelmed the Titans' defenses. At the same time, Zeus called down every lightning bolt he could summon. The sky turned white with electricity. The ground melted into glass.

The Titans broke. They tried to retreat, but the Olympians were everywhere. Poseidon's earthquakes prevented any escape. Hades appeared from nowhere to cut off routes. Zeus's thunderbolts drove them back.

One by one, the Titans fell. Zeus bound them in chains forged by the Cyclopes—chains that no immortal could break. Then he opened Tartarus and hurled them in.

Zeus dealt harshly with the leaders. Cronus, the father who'd swallowed his children, was cast into the deepest part of Tartarus. Atlas, the general of the Titan army, received a special punishment. Zeus forced him to hold up the sky on his shoulders for all eternity, standing at the western edge of the world, bearing the weight of the heavens alone.

Menoetius was struck by a thunderbolt and cast into Erebus for his arrogance. The other rebel Titans joined Cronus in Tartarus. The Hecatoncheires became their jailers, standing guard to ensure they never escaped.

But Zeus showed mercy to some. Oceanus, who'd stayed neutral, kept his river realm. Themis was honored for her wisdom and became an advisor. Prometheus, who'd fought for the Olympians, was elevated to a high status, though that relationship would sour later.

The war was over. The old order had fallen, and a new generation ruled the cosmos.

Zeus and his brothers drew lots to divide the universe fairly. Zeus won the sky and became king of the gods. Poseidon took the seas and all waters. Hades received the underworld and the dead. The Earth and Mount Olympus would be shared territory—neutral ground where all three could walk. But Zeus clearly held the most power. He had the thunderbolt. He had led the war. He was king.

However, the cycle of violence that had defined both Uranus's and Cronus's reigns would continue to haunt this new generation. Zeus had won his throne through rebellion and war, but that throne would never be entirely secure. He would face challenges from the Giants, Typhon, and even his own wife. The cosmos would never be completely at peace.

From Chaos came order. From order came conflict. From conflict came a new order. This was the pattern of Greek creation—not a gentle unfolding, but a violent struggle between generations, each overthrowing the last. Not a world created by a benevolent designer, but one torn from Chaos through force, cunning, and blood.

And at the center of it all stood Zeus, king of the gods, wielder of the thunderbolt, ruler of Olympus. But before Zeus could truly rule in peace, he would face two massive challenges.

A statue of Zeus with his thunderbolt.[3]

The Final Threats:
Typhon and the Gigantomachy

Victory over the Titans didn't mean the war was over. Gaia, the Earth herself, was furious. Her Titan children had been cast into Tartarus. Her grandson, Zeus, had won through violence and cunning. She had helped orchestrate the fall of both Uranus and Cronus, but now she turned against Zeus too. The cycle of vengeance would continue.

Gaia's first move was to give birth to one final child—the most terrifying monster the cosmos had ever seen. His name was Typhon (or Typhoeus), and he was designed to destroy Zeus and everything the Olympians had built.

Typhon was colossal. Ancient sources disagree on his exact appearance, but all agree he was nightmarish. Some say he was so tall his head brushed the stars. Others describe him as having a hundred dragon heads, each breathing fire and speaking in different voices. His body was covered in scales. His arms, when stretched out, reached from the eastern to the western horizon. Instead of legs, he had massive serpent coils. His eyes blazed with fire. When he moved, the earth shook.

Typhon erupted from the earth and immediately attacked Olympus.

The gods panicked. This wasn't like fighting the Titans, disciplined, strategic opponents who could be outmaneuvered. This was pure chaos and destruction given form. Many of the gods fled. Some accounts say they ran all the way to Egypt and disguised themselves as animals to hide. Only Zeus stood his ground.

The battle between Zeus and Typhon shook the universe. Zeus hurled thunderbolts, but Typhon shrugged them off. The monster grabbed mountains and threw them. He breathed fire that scorched the heavens. The earth melted beneath their feet, and the seas boiled. Even Tartarus trembled. The imprisoned Titans thought they might be freed by the destruction above.

In some versions, Typhon actually won the first round. He overpowered Zeus, wrestled him to the ground, and cut the tendons from his hands and feet, crippling the king of the gods. He dragged Zeus to a cave in Cilicia and left him there, helpless and guarded by a dragon. Hermes, the messenger god, and Pan, the god of the wild and shepherds, eventually rescued Zeus, stealing back his tendons and restoring his strength.

The rematch was decisive. Zeus attacked with every thunderbolt he could summon, hitting Typhon again and again. The monster's hundred heads caught fire. His scales melted. His strength failed. Finally, Zeus lifted Mount Etna—the massive volcano in Sicily—and hurled it on top of Typhon, trapping him forever.

To this day, Mount Etna still erupts. The Greeks said that it was Typhon trying to escape his prison. Every earthquake in the region was Typhon shifting his weight. Every volcanic eruption was his rage.

With Typhon defeated, Zeus had proven his power beyond question. But Gaia wasn't finished.

She stirred up the Giants, those beings born from Uranus's blood when Cronus castrated him. The Giants were enormous warriors. They were as tall as mountains, immensely strong, and difficult to kill. They wore armor made from animal skins and wielded massive clubs, boulders, and even whole trees torn from the earth.

The Giants declared war on the Olympians. This conflict, the Gigantomachy, was different from the Titanomachy. The Titans had been gods fighting gods. The Giants were monstrous, savage, and driven by pure rage against the Olympian order.

The Giants had one significant advantage: they couldn't be killed by gods alone. A prophecy stated that the Giants could only be destroyed if a god and a mortal worked together to strike them down. The gods needed human help.

This is where Heracles enters the story. Though he wouldn't be born until much later in the mythological timeline, many sources place him at the Gigantomachy. The timeline gets fuzzy here because Greek myths weren't concerned with chronological consistency. What mattered was that Heracles, the greatest of all mortal heroes, fought alongside the gods.

The battle was massive. The Giants attacked Olympus itself, piling mountain on top of mountain to create a ramp to heaven. They hurled boulders and flaming trees. They were relentless.

Athena fought brilliantly, using strategy as much as strength. She killed the Giant Pallas and later wore his skin as a cloak, which is why she's sometimes called Pallas Athena. She also defeated Enceladus by throwing the entire island of Sicily on top of him. Like Typhon, he remained trapped beneath, causing earthquakes when he struggled.

Apollo shot the Giant Ephialtes with arrows. Poseidon broke off part of the island of Kos and crushed the Giant Polybotes beneath it. Dionysus killed Eurytus with his thyrsus (a staff wrapped in ivy). Hephaestus threw molten metal at the Giants. Even Hades joined the fight, using his helmet of invisibility to strike unseen.

But in each case, it was Heracles who delivered the killing blow. The gods would wound a Giant, and Heracles would finish them off with his arrows. Without him, the Giants would simply have regenerated and continued fighting.

The most dangerous Giant was Alcyoneus. He was immortal as long as he remained in his homeland. Heracles realized this, so he wrestled him and dragged him beyond his territory's borders. Once separated from his land, Alcyoneus became mortal, and Heracles killed him.

Another formidable Giant was Porphyrion, who attacked Hera herself. Zeus struck him with a thunderbolt to protect his wife, and Heracles finished him with an arrow through the heart.

One by one, the Giants fell. The gods and Heracles fought for days, maybe years. The earth ran red with immortal blood. Mountains were shattered. Islands were created from the stones thrown during the battle.

Finally, the last Giant was killed. The Olympians had won. Gaia's rebellion had failed, though she never quite forgave Zeus. She would occasionally send other monsters or support other challengers to Olympian rule, but she would never again mount a full-scale war.

Zeus and the Olympians were now secure. They had defeated the Titans, the greatest monster ever born, and an army of Giants. The cosmic order was established. Zeus's throne was unshakable.

Or so it seemed. Because while the external threats were defeated, the Olympians would create plenty of internal problems on their own. Zeus's infidelity would spark conflicts. The gods' pride would lead to disaster. Their interference in mortal affairs would cause wars that lasted decades.

But all of that was still to come. For now, Zeus stood triumphant on Mount Olympus, surrounded by his siblings and the new generation of gods. The age of heroes was approaching. Humanity was about to be created. And the stories that we still tell today were about to begin.

Chapter 2: The Big Three and the Olympic Court

With the Titans defeated and the cosmos divided, the Olympian gods established their rule on Mount Olympus. This wasn't a democracy. It wasn't even a fair monarchy. It was a divine oligarchy run by a dysfunctional family with infinite power and very little impulse control.

The twelve Olympians lived on the peak of Mount Olympus, the highest mountain in Greece. They feasted on ambrosia and nectar, which sustained their immortality. They meddled in human affairs. They fought with each other constantly. And they created most of the drama that would define Greek mythology.

Let's meet the family.

Zeus: The King of the Gods

Zeus won the lottery—literally. After defeating the Titans, he and his brothers Poseidon and Hades drew lots to divide the universe. Zeus got the sky, which made him king.

But Zeus wasn't just lucky. He was clever, ruthless when necessary, and understood power better than anyone. He'd orchestrated the rebellion against Cronus. He'd freed the Cyclopes and Hecatoncheires, securing their loyalty. He'd wielded the thunderbolt in battle. When the dust settled, his siblings recognized him as their leader, not just because he won the sky but because he'd secured the throne through superior alliances and overwhelming firepower.

Zeus ruled from a throne on Mount Olympus. His symbols were the thunderbolt, the eagle, and the oak tree. His weapon could crack mountains, kill immortals, and level cities. When Zeus was angry, the sky itself became dangerous. Thunder announced his displeasure. Lightning struck those who offended him.

But Zeus's real power wasn't the thunderbolt. It was his ability to maintain order among beings who couldn't be controlled by force alone. The other Olympians were immortal and nearly as powerful as he was. He couldn't rule them through fear. He had to use politics, alliances, compromises, and intimidation.

Zeus also served as the ultimate judge. Mortals who wanted justice appealed to Zeus. Kings claimed to rule by his authority. Oaths sworn in Zeus's name were binding; breaking them brought his wrath. The Greeks gave him multiple titles reflecting these roles: protector of guests and strangers (hospitality was sacred), god of oaths, and protector of those who begged for mercy.

But Zeus had a massive flaw: he couldn't keep it in his pants.

His wife was Hera, his sister and the queen of the gods. However, Zeus had countless affairs with goddesses, nymphs, and mortal women. He fathered dozens of children. Some even became major gods (Athena, Apollo, Artemis, Hermes, Dionysus, and Persephone were all his children), and others became legendary heroes (like Heracles, Perseus, and Helen of Troy). He transformed to seduce women, becoming a swan, a bull, and even a shower of gold. Sometimes he tricked them. Sometimes he forced them.

Leda and Zeus (as a swan).'

These weren't romantic love stories. The Greeks viewed these as divine seizures or fated events, but by any modern standard, many were acts of violence that we would recognize as assault today. The myths don't apologize for this or explain it away. Zeus was the king of the gods, and he did what he wanted. Even the king of heaven was deeply flawed.

His infidelity caused massive problems. Hera was furious at being constantly humiliated, and she took revenge on Zeus's lovers and illegitimate children. She couldn't punish Zeus directly, as he was too powerful. So, she punished everyone else. This cycle of Zeus's affairs and Hera's revenge drives many of the most famous Greek myths.

Zeus's relationship with humanity was complicated. He didn't particularly like humans; they were weak, short-lived, and troublesome. But he couldn't ignore them either. They offered sacrifices and built temples. They invoked his name in oaths and prayers. And sometimes, very occasionally, Zeus fell in love with a mortal woman and produced a child who would change history.

The Zeus we see in the myths isn't all-knowing or all-good. He makes mistakes. He's deceived by other gods. He's swayed by flattery and anger. He can be cruel, petty, and vindictive. But he's also capable of wisdom, justice, and mercy when the mood strikes him.

And that made him more interesting than any perfect deity could be.

Poseidon and Hades:
The Division of the Universe

Zeus's brothers got different domains, but calling them "short ends of the stick" isn't quite right.

Poseidon received the seas, all waters, and earthquakes. Hades got the underworld and the dead. While the sky was the most visible domain and came with the kingship, each brother inherited a kingdom of absolute power. Poseidon ruled more of the earth's surface than Zeus. Hades ruled over every soul that ever died or would die. In terms of subjects, Hades had the largest kingdom by far.

Poseidon: Lord of the Seas

Poseidon was the second most powerful Olympian. He was temperamental and vindictive, holding grudges that could last for decades. His symbol was the trident, a three-pronged spear that could create earthquakes and storms and split rocks to release springs of water.

The Greeks called earthquakes "earth-shakers," and they attributed them to Poseidon striking the ground with his trident. This made him terrifying. Earthquakes destroyed cities, collapsed temples, and killed thousands. Poseidon's anger could reshape coastlines.

He lived in an underwater palace made of coral and gems. He drove a chariot pulled by hippocampi, creatures that were half-horse, half-fish. He ruled over all sea creatures and could command the waves themselves.

Poseidon desperately wanted more power on land. He competed with other gods for the patronage of cities. His most famous rivalry was with Athena over Athens.

Both gods wanted to be the city's patron deity. The Athenians decided to hold a contest. Each god would give the city a gift, and the citizens would choose which was more valuable.

The contest took place on the Acropolis, the high rocky outcrop that dominated Athens. Poseidon went first. He struck the rock with his trident, and water gushed forth. It seemed impressive, especially since water was precious. But the water was salty and undrinkable, making it worthless for a city that needed fresh water.

Athena went next. She struck the ground with her spear, and an olive tree grew. This was the first olive tree in the world. The olive tree provided food, oil for lamps, oil for cooking, wood for building, and economic value through trade. It was practical, sustainable, and brilliant.

The citizens chose Athena. The city was named Athens in her honor.

Poseidon was furious. He flooded the Thriasian Plain surrounding Athens in revenge, destroying crops and homes. The Athenians had to offer sacrifices to appease him. Even after that, Poseidon remained bitter about losing Athens. This pattern repeated elsewhere. When Hera beat him for patronage of Argos, he dried up the region's rivers out of spite.

Poseidon also created horses, according to most traditions. In one version, he created the first horse while competing with Athena for Athens, but the judges preferred her olive tree anyway. In another version, he created horses while pursuing Demeter. She turned into a mare to escape. He became a stallion and caught her anyway. From that union came the immortal horse Arion and, in some versions, the goddess Despoina.

Horses were sacred to Poseidon. Before sea voyages, sailors would sacrifice horses to him. These would have been expensive offerings, showing their desperation for safe passage. Horse races were held in his honor. The Isthmian Games, second only in popularity to the Olympics, were dedicated to Poseidon.

Poseidon's offspring reflected his violent nature. He fathered Theseus, the hero of Athens (ironic, given his hatred of the city). He fathered Polyphemus, the Cyclops who ate Odysseus's men. He fathered the hunter Orion, who was eventually killed by Artemis. He fathered numerous giants and monsters who terrorized humanity.

His son Chrysaor and grandson Geryon (a three-bodied giant) both died

A colossal statue of Poseidon.[5]

fighting Heracles. His son Antaeus was a giant who grew stronger whenever he touched the earth. Heracles killed him by lifting him off the ground and crushing him in a bear hug.

Poseidon supported the Greeks during the Trojan War, but not for noble reasons. Troy's founder had cheated Poseidon out of payment for building the city's walls. Poseidon held that grudge for generations and used the war as his chance for revenge.

His temper was legendary. When Odysseus blinded Polyphemus, Poseidon made Odysseus's journey home take ten years and killed all his men. When the Phaeacians helped Odysseus, Poseidon turned their ship to stone as it returned home. When King Minos of Crete refused to sacrifice a beautiful white bull Poseidon had sent, the god made Minos's wife, Pasiphaë, fall in love with the bull. Their offspring was the Minotaur.

The sea was Poseidon's personality—beautiful and calm one moment and violently destructive the next. You couldn't predict him. You couldn't control him. You could only pray you didn't anger him.

The sea was life and death to the Greeks. They were traders, colonizers, and warriors who spent months on the water. Poseidon controlled their fate. That made him one of the most worshiped gods despite not being the king.

Hades: The Unseen One

Hades got the worst deal in the cosmic lottery. He became lord of the underworld, ruler of the dead, and keeper of the souls who would never see sunlight again.

But here's the thing. Hades wasn't evil. He was just doing his job.

Unlike the Christian concept of hell, where the dead are punished constantly, the Greek underworld was mostly boring. Only the truly wicked went to Tartarus for punishment. Only the greatest heroes went to the Elysian Fields as a reward. Everyone else went to the Asphodel Meadows, a gray, shadowy place where they wandered forever as shades. They didn't face torture or fire—just an endless, dreary existence.

Hades rarely left his realm. He had no interest in Olympus or the politics of the living gods. He wore a helmet that made him invisible—the same helmet the Cyclopes had forged during the war with the Titans. His symbols were the cypress tree, the narcissus flower, and the screech owl.

The Greeks were so afraid of attracting Hades's attention that they rarely spoke his name. They called him "the Unseen One" or "the Rich One" (because all the earth's mineral wealth was in his domain). Saying "Hades" was considered unlucky because you might remind him that you existed, and then he'd come for you.

Hades had one major myth, the abduction of Persephone, which we'll cover in detail shortly. Otherwise, he mostly appeared in myths when heroes descended to the underworld and had to deal with him. He was stern, inflexible, and fair. He made no exceptions. When your time came, you went to Hades.

Hades and Persephone.[6]

He didn't hate the living, and he didn't torture souls for fun. He just maintained order in the realm of the dead. In a way, Hades was the most responsible of the three brothers. Zeus couldn't keep his affairs straight. Poseidon threw tantrums and flooded cities. Hades did his job quietly and efficiently.

The Greeks respected Hades but didn't worship him much. Why would you? You couldn't ask him for favors. He didn't grant wishes. He didn't answer prayers for good weather or successful harvests. He just waited for everyone to eventually die and join him.

In later Christian-influenced interpretations, Hades became confused with Satan. In those accounts, he was a cosmic evil who ruled over punishment and suffering. But that's not the Greek Hades. The Greek Hades was neutral. Death wasn't a punishment. It was just the inevitable end.

The Queens of Olympus:
Hera's Power and Hestia's Hearth

The female Olympians don't get as much attention in modern retellings, but they were just as important as their male counterparts. Let's start with the two oldest: Hera and Hestia.

Hera: Queen of Heaven and Goddess of Marriage

Hera was Zeus's wife and the queen of the gods. Her symbols were the peacock, the cow, and the pomegranate. She was the goddess of marriage, women, childbirth, and family.

This is deeply ironic because her own marriage was a disaster.

Hera was Zeus's sister. She was the daughter of Cronus and Rhea. She had been swallowed and later freed. Zeus pursued her romantically, but she initially refused him. In one version, Zeus transformed into a bedraggled cuckoo bird. Hera, feeling sorry for the bird, held it to her breast to warm it. Zeus immediately transformed back and, depending on the version, either seduced or forced himself on her. Shamed, Hera agreed to marry him.

Their marriage was the model for all marriages, which tells you something about Greek views on marriage. It wasn't about love. It was about duty, alliance, and maintaining social order.

Hera took her role as goddess of marriage seriously. She punished those who violated marriage vows or insulted the institution. But she couldn't punish Zeus for his constant infidelity; he was too powerful. So, she punished his lovers instead.

For instance, she forbade any land from giving Leto a place to give birth (Leto finally found refuge on the floating island of Delos). She tricked Semele into asking to see Zeus's true form, which incinerated her. And she hated Heracles, Zeus's son by Alcmene, from birth, eventually driving him mad and causing him to murder his own family. The famous Twelve Labors were Heracles's penance for murders that Hera had caused.

She participated in the Trojan War on the side of the Greeks because Paris, the Trojan prince, had judged Aphrodite more beautiful than her in a divine beauty contest. Hera held that grudge for ten years and helped orchestrate the destruction of Troy.

But Hera wasn't just vengeful. She was also powerful, dignified, and commanded respect. She had her own cult following, especially among married women who prayed to her for protection in childbirth and harmony in marriage.

Hera embodied a harsh truth. In Greek society, women had power only within very limited spheres. Hera couldn't control her husband, so she controlled what she could—other women, children, and her own reputation. She was trapped in a marriage that humiliated her constantly, and she dealt with it the only way she could.

Modern readers often dislike Hera. She seems cruel, petty, and jealous. But in context, she's a woman fighting back with the only weapons available to her. She couldn't divorce Zeus. She couldn't kill him. She couldn't even publicly shame him since he was king. So, she survived by making everyone else as miserable as he made her.

Hestia: The Hearth Goddess

Hestia was the firstborn child of Cronus and Rhea, so she was the first to be swallowed and the last to be freed. By rights, she should have been important. However, she chose a different path.

Hestia was the goddess of the hearth, home, and domestic life. Her symbol was the hearth fire, the flame that burned in the center of every Greek home and in the center of every city's public hall.

She was a virgin goddess, having sworn an oath of eternal chastity. Both Poseidon and Apollo pursued her romantically, but she refused them both. Zeus, respecting her choice, granted her a place of honor. She would receive the first offering at every sacrifice.

This wasn't a small thing. In Greek religion, the order of offerings mattered. Hestia getting the first offering meant she was honored above all others. But she never demanded worship, never caused problems, and never appeared in dramatic myths. She existed peacefully, keeping homes warm and families fed.

In many ways, Hestia represented the opposite of the dramatic, violent gods around her. While Zeus hurled lightning and Poseidon flooded cities, Hestia maintained the quiet, steady flame that made civilization possible.

Later, Hestia would give up her seat among the twelve Olympians to Dionysus to avoid conflict. This is very much in character—she avoided drama.

The Greeks weren't great at keeping a consistent roster of the twelve Olympians. In some lists, Hestia is included. In others, Dionysus replaces her. Both versions existed simultaneously in Greek religion. The number twelve mattered more than the specific names.

Hestia never married, never had children, and never started wars. By the standards of Greek mythology, this made her boring. But it also made her essential. Every Greek home had a hearth. Every sacrifice began with an offering to Hestia. She was the most worshiped and least celebrated of the gods.

Demeter and the Seasons: The Abduction of Persephone and Why Winter Exists

Demeter was the goddess of agriculture, grain, and the harvest. She made crops grow and ensured the fertility of the earth. She was absolutely crucial to human survival in an agricultural society.

Her most famous myth explains the seasons and reveals the cost of divine politics.

Demeter had a daughter named Persephone (also called Kore, meaning "maiden"). Zeus was her father.

Persephone was considered beautiful and innocent. One day, she was gathering narcissus flowers in a meadow when the ground split open.

Hades emerged from the underworld, driving a chariot pulled by black horses. He grabbed Persephone and dragged her down into his realm before she could even scream. The earth closed behind them.

Why did Hades abduct her? Some versions say he had fallen in love. Others say he wanted a queen, and Persephone was a logical choice. Some later sources claim Zeus had promised Persephone to

A modern restoration of a statue of Demeter.[7]

Hades without telling Demeter or asking Persephone. Regardless, Persephone was taken against her will.

Demeter heard her daughter's scream from far away. She ran to the meadow, but Persephone was gone. No one would tell Demeter what had happened. The gods looked away. The nymphs claimed they saw nothing.

Demeter searched for nine days and nine nights, carrying torches when it grew too dark. She did not eat or sleep. Finally, the goddess Hecate, who had heard the scream, told her what direction it had come from. Helios, the sun god who sees everything, revealed the truth: Hades had taken Persephone to be his queen.

Demeter was devastated. She abandoned Olympus in her grief and rage. Disguised as an old woman, she wandered the earth. She came to Eleusis, where the king and queen took her in as a nursemaid for their infant son.

Demeter grew to love the child and decided to make him immortal. Every night, she placed him in the fire to burn away his mortality. But one night, the queen walked in and screamed in horror at seeing her baby in the flames. Demeter, interrupted, revealed her true form. The child would now remain mortal. But Demeter taught the people of Eleusis the mysteries of agriculture and established her cult there. The famous Eleusinian Mysteries would last for thousands of years.

Demeter was still upset about her daughter. She refused to let anything grow. Crops failed. Trees died. The earth became barren. Humans began to starve. If this continued, humanity would go extinct, and the gods would lose their worshipers and sacrifices.

Zeus sent messengers to Demeter, begging her to relent. She refused. She would not restore the earth until she got her daughter back.

Zeus had no choice. He ordered Hades to return Persephone.

Hades agreed, but with a trick. Before Persephone left, he offered her pomegranate seeds. In some versions, she ate them willingly. In others, he tricked her. Either way, she consumed food from the underworld—and anyone who ate in the underworld was bound to it forever.

Persephone returned to the surface. Demeter was overjoyed. But Hermes, the messenger god, delivered the bad news. Persephone had eaten six pomegranate seeds. She was bound to Hades.

After negotiation, a compromise was reached. Persephone would spend part of the year with Hades in the underworld and part with Demeter on earth. The usual version says six months with each, corresponding to the six seeds she ate, though different Greek regions had different ideas about how long winter lasted and adjusted the story accordingly.

This is the Greek explanation for the seasons. When Persephone is with Demeter, the earth blooms. Spring and summer arrive. Demeter is happy, so crops grow, and the world is fertile. But when Persephone descends to the underworld, Demeter grieves. Autumn and winter come. Nothing grows, and the earth mourns.

The myth is about many things. It's about the changing seasons. It's about a mother's love for her daughter. It's about the powerlessness of even goddesses when male gods make decisions about their lives. It's about loss, grief, and the compromises we make to survive.

Persephone herself is an interesting figure. In the underworld, she became queen and ruled alongside Hades. Some later sources suggest she grew to love him or at least accepted her role. She became a powerful goddess who judged the dead and sometimes granted favors to heroes who descended to Hades's realm.

But every year, she returned to her mother. And every year, the cycle repeated.

The "Middle Management": Profiles with Signature Myths

Athena: Wisdom Born from Violence

Athena was Zeus's favorite child, and her birth was appropriately dramatic.

Zeus had an affair with Metis, the Titaness of wisdom and cunning. When Metis became pregnant, Zeus received a prophecy. Metis would bear two children. The first would be a daughter equal to Zeus in wisdom. The second would be a son who would overthrow Zeus, just as Zeus had overthrown Cronus, and Cronus had overthrown Uranus.

Zeus, learning nothing from his father's mistakes, decided to prevent this prophecy. He swallowed Metis whole while she was still pregnant.

Time passed. Zeus developed a splitting headache. The pain was unbearable. He called for Hephaestus, the smith god, and ordered him to split his head open with an ax.

A Roman copy of a Greek statue of Athena.[8]

Hephaestus obliged. He struck Zeus's skull with a mighty blow, and from the wound emerged Athena fully grown, fully armed, wearing golden armor and a helmet, holding a spear, and screaming a war cry that shook Olympus.

The Greeks considered Metis her mother and Zeus her father, even though the actual birth happened from Zeus's head. Swallowing the mother didn't get rid of Athena's maternal lineage—it just made for a very strange birth story. She was wisdom incarnate. She became the goddess of war (specifically strategic warfare, as opposed to Ares's chaotic bloodlust), crafts, and wisdom.

Athens claimed her as its patron goddess, and she became the most important deity in that city. The Parthenon, one of the most famous temples ever built, was dedicated to Athena Parthenos (Athena the Virgin). She was a virgin goddess, like Hestia and Artemis, having sworn never to marry.

Athena's wisdom made her invaluable. Heroes constantly sought her help. Odysseus was her favorite, as she loved his cleverness. She helped Perseus kill Medusa by giving him a polished shield to use as a mirror. She helped Heracles complete his labors. She fought in the Trojan War on the side of the Greeks.

But Athena could be cruel. When the mortal weaver Arachne boasted she could weave better than Athena, the goddess challenged her to a contest. Arachne's tapestry was perfect, possibly even better than Athena's. It also depicted the gods' various infidelities and crimes. Athena was furious. She struck Arachne and destroyed her work. Arachne, in despair, hanged herself. Athena transformed her into a spider, dooming her to weave forever.

Apollo and Artemis: Twin Powers

Apollo and Artemis were the twin children of Zeus and the Titaness Leto. Their birth was difficult because Hera, jealous as always, forbade any land from giving Leto shelter. Finally, the floating island of Delos allowed her to give birth.

Apollo was the god of music, poetry, prophecy, healing, archery, and the sun, though Helios was technically the sun god (Apollo became associated with it later). He was beautiful and talented, and he knew it. He played the lyre perfectly. His arrows never missed. And he controlled the most important oracle in all of Greece.

The Oracle at Delphi was Apollo's greatest power source. Delphi sat on the slopes of Mount Parnassus, which was considered the center of the world. The Greeks believed Zeus had released two eagles from opposite ends of the earth, and they met at Delphi, marking it as the world's navel (*omphalos*).

Originally, the site belonged to Gaia and was guarded by the monstrous serpent Python. Apollo, only a few days old, came to Delphi and killed Python with his arrows. He then claimed the oracle for himself. The Pythia, the priestess who delivered prophecies, sat on a tripod above a chasm in the earth. Vapors rose from the chasm (possibly natural gases from geological activity), and she breathed them in, entering a trance. In this state, she channeled Apollo's prophecies.

The Oracle's pronouncements shaped Greek history. Kings consulted the Oracle before wars. Colonists asked where to found new cities. Individuals sought guidance on major decisions. The prophecies were famously ambiguous. When King Croesus of Lydia asked if he should attack Persia, the Oracle said, "If you cross the river, a great empire will fall." Croesus attacked. A great empire did fall—his own.

When Oedipus's father consulted the Oracle, he was told his son would kill him and marry his wife. Every attempt to prevent this prophecy only ensured it came true. Apollo's prophecies were always accurate but rarely clear.

Apollo's love life was consistently tragic. He fell in love with the nymph Daphne, who wanted nothing to do with him. The story usually says Eros shot Apollo with a golden arrow of love and Daphne with a lead arrow of revulsion in revenge for Apollo mocking Eros's archery skills. Apollo chased Daphne relentlessly. She ran until she couldn't run anymore, then prayed to her father, the river god Peneus, for help. He transformed her into a laurel tree. Apollo, unable to have her as a wife, declared the laurel his sacred tree and wore a laurel crown forever after. Athletic victors at the Pythian Games (held in Apollo's honor) received laurel wreaths.

He loved the Spartan prince Hyacinthus, and they were happy together. One day, while throwing the discus, Apollo's throw went wide. Some say the West Wind, Zephyrus, jealous of their love, blew it off course. The discus struck Hyacinthus in the head and killed him instantly. Apollo tried desperately to heal him, but even gods can't reverse death. From Hyacinthus's spilled blood grew the hyacinth flower, its petals marked with Apollo's cries of grief.

He loved the prophetess Cassandra and gave her the gift of prophecy. But when she refused to sleep with him, he couldn't take back a divine gift, so he cursed it. Cassandra would still see the future accurately, but no one would ever believe her. She foresaw the fall of Troy. She warned about the Trojan Horse. No one listened.

Apollo could be petty and cruel. When the satyr Marsyas challenged him to a musical contest, Apollo won (the Muses judged, and they wouldn't dare offend an Olympian). Apollo's punishment for Marsyas's presumption was horrific. He flayed Marsyas alive, peeling off his skin while he screamed. The satyrs and woodland creatures wept so much that their tears formed the river Marsyas.

But Apollo also represented civilization's highest achievements. He led the Muses, the nine goddesses of arts and sciences. Poetry, astronomy, history, tragedy, and comedy flourished under Apollo's patronage. The greatest poets and musicians honored Apollo. Plato called philosophy a form of music in Apollo's service.

Apollo embodied the Greek ideal of moderation and rational thought. His temple at Delphi bore the inscriptions "Know Thyself" and "Nothing in Excess." He represented the controlled, civilized side of human nature—everything Dionysus wasn't.

Apollo and his twin sister Artemis were fiercely protective of each other and their mother. When the Giant Tityos attempted to rape Leto, the twins killed him with arrows and sent him to Tartarus for eternal punishment.

When Queen Niobe boasted that she was a better mother than Leto because she had fourteen children while Leto had only two, Apollo and Artemis killed all fourteen of Niobe's children with arrows. Niobe was transformed into stone, forever weeping for her dead children.

Artemis was the goddess of the hunt, wild animals, the wilderness, childbirth, and young women. Like Athena and Hestia, she was a virgin goddess who swore never to marry or have relations with any man. She led a band of hunting nymphs who had also sworn off men and dedicated themselves to the hunt.

Artemis was fiercely independent and protective of her and her followers' virginity. When Zeus raped one of her nymphs, Callisto, Artemis discovered she was pregnant and expelled her from the group. Hera then transformed Callisto into a bear. Years later, Callisto's son, Arcas, nearly killed her while hunting, not recognizing his own mother.

Zeus, feeling guilty, placed both of them in the sky as the constellations Ursa Major (Great Bear) and Ursa Minor (Little Bear).

Artemis demanded absolute loyalty from her followers. When one of her nymphs, Opis, caught the eye of the river god Alpheus, Artemis helped her escape by disguising all her nymphs (including herself) with mud so they all looked identical. Artemis protected her own.

The hunter Actaeon made a fatal mistake. While hunting with his dogs, he stumbled upon a grotto where Artemis was bathing naked with her nymphs. Accounts differ on whether it was accidental or deliberate. Either way, Artemis was furious. She transformed him into a stag. His own hunting dogs, not recognizing their master, tore him apart and ate him.

King Agamemnon made an even worse mistake. While hunting, he killed a deer in Artemis's sacred grove and boasted, "Not even Artemis could have made that shot." Artemis was furious at his hubris. When Agamemnon prepared to sail to Troy with the Greek fleet, Artemis sent winds that prevented the ships from leaving. The prophet Calchas revealed that Artemis demanded a sacrifice: Agamemnon's own daughter, Iphigenia.

In most versions, Agamemnon lured Iphigenia to the camp under the pretense that she would marry Achilles. When he placed her on the altar and raised the knife, Artemis (in some versions) took pity and substituted a deer at the last moment, spiriting Iphigenia away to serve as a priestess in Tauris. In other versions, the sacrifice happened. Either way, Artemis made her point: respect the goddess of the hunt, or pay the price.

Artemis's relationship with the hunter Orion is told in several contradictory versions. In one, Orion joined Artemis's hunt and became her companion. Some sources suggest she fell in love with him, though she would never admit it. Apollo, protective of his sister's virginity and worried she would break her vow, tricked her. He pointed to a distant target in the sea and challenged Artemis to hit it with an arrow. Artemis, never one to back down from a challenge, shot the target perfectly. When she swam out to retrieve her kill, she discovered it was Orion. Devastated, she placed him among the stars as the constellation Orion.

In another version, Orion tried to rape Artemis or one of her followers. She sent a giant scorpion to kill him. Both Orion and the scorpion were placed in the sky as constellations, forever chasing each other across the heavens.

In yet another version, Orion boasted he would hunt and kill every animal on earth. Gaia, offended, sent the scorpion to stop him.

The contradictions matter less than the themes. Artemis was deadly, untouchable, and utterly dedicated to the wilderness and the hunt. She represented freedom from civilization and from men.

Paradoxically, Artemis was also the goddess of childbirth. This likely stems from her role as the protector of young women and her association with her mother's difficult labor. Women in childbirth prayed to Artemis for an easy delivery.

Where Apollo represented civilization, music, and rational thought, Artemis represented wild nature, instinct, and independence. Together, the twins embodied both balance and tension. Apollo built cities; Artemis roamed the wilderness. Apollo gathered people; Artemis scattered them. They loved each other fiercely and defended each other without question, but they were opposites in almost every way.

Ares and Aphrodite: The Affair

Aphrodite was the goddess of love, beauty, sex, and desire. Her power was immense, perhaps greater than any other deity's. Zeus could hurl thunderbolts, but Aphrodite could make Zeus himself fall helplessly in love. Ares represented war, but Aphrodite could start wars with a glance. She controlled the fundamental force that drove gods and mortals alike.

Her birth story was extraordinary. Remember when Cronus castrated Uranus and threw the severed genitals into the sea? Those genitals drifted on the waves, and white foam gathered around them. From that foam, Aphrodite emerged fully grown, impossibly beautiful, and standing on a scallop shell. The West Wind blew her to shore on the island of Cyprus (or Cythera, depending on the version). Where her feet touched the earth, flowers bloomed.

This made Aphrodite ancient. She was older than the Olympians and born from the primal violence that ended Uranus's reign. Some later sources tried to make her Zeus's daughter by the Titaness Dione, probably to fit her into the Olympian family tree more neatly. But the older, stranger version was the one most Greeks knew.

Her beauty was literally irresistible. When she walked into a room, conversations stopped. Men lost their minds. Gods fell at her feet. She wore a magical girdle that made whomever she desired fall in love with her. No one could resist Aphrodite when she decided to seduce them.

Zeus arranged her marriage to Hephaestus, the god of the forge, metalworking, and craftsmanship, probably hoping to bind her to someone stable. Aphrodite hated it. She didn't want to be married to someone she considered ugly and boring. She wanted excitement, passion, danger.

She found it with Ares, the god of war.

Ares was everything Hephaestus wasn't. He was violent, passionate, handsome, and exciting. Ares was also foolish and impulsive, but Aphrodite didn't care. Their affair was passionate and reckless. They didn't even try to hide it particularly well.

One day, Helios, the sun god (who sees everything), told Hephaestus what was happening. Hephaestus was devastated and furious. But he was also clever. He forged a magical net that was invisible, unbreakable, and finer than spider silk. He set it as a trap over his and Aphrodite's bed.

The next time Ares and Aphrodite met for an encounter, the net sprang. They were caught mid-act, completely naked, and unable to escape.

Hephaestus called all the gods to come see. The male gods came and laughed at Ares's humiliation. The goddesses, embarrassed, stayed away. Ares and Aphrodite were trapped until Poseidon convinced Hephaestus to free them.

Ares slunk away in shame. Aphrodite fled to Cyprus. Their affair continued, but they were more careful.

The affair represented something the Greeks understood: love and war are intertwined. Aphrodite and Ares embodied the destructive, irrational passions that drive people. From their union came several children, including Eros (in some traditions—remember there was also a primordial Eros), Phobos (Fear), and Deimos (Terror), who accompanied Ares into battle. They also had a daughter, Harmonia, who represented the harmony that can come after conflict.

Aphrodite had other lovers too. She had an extended affair with the mortal shepherd Anchises and bore him a son, Aeneas, who would survive the fall of Troy and become the legendary founder of Rome. She loved the beautiful youth Adonis so much that she fought with Persephone over who got to keep him. Zeus had to mediate, declaring that Adonis would spend part of the year with each goddess. While hunting, Adonis was killed by a wild boar (sent either by the jealous Ares or by Artemis, depending on the version). Aphrodite's tears mixed with his blood and created the anemone flower.

Aphrodite could be generous or vindictive, depending on whether you honored or insulted her. When the women of Lemnos failed to honor her properly, she cursed them with a terrible smell that drove their husbands away. When Hippolytus, a devotee of Artemis, scorned love and mocked Aphrodite, she made his stepmother, Phaedra, fall desperately in love with him. This led to a tragedy that destroyed the entire family.

Aphrodite represented desire in all its forms—creative and destructive, beautiful and terrible. She could bring joy or devastation. She made you feel alive, but she could also destroy everything you'd built. The Greeks knew that desire was dangerous. They worshiped Aphrodite out of respect and fear, knowing that everyone—god or mortal—was vulnerable to her power.

Ares was the god of war. He represented violence, bloodlust, and chaos. The Greeks didn't particularly like Ares. He represented the worst parts of war: the mindless slaughter, the brutality, the madness. Ares was often a loser in mythology; he lost almost every fight he participated in. Even mortals sometimes beat him.

He was Zeus's son by Hera, but even his parents didn't like him much. In the *Iliad*, when Ares is wounded in battle, he runs crying to Zeus. Zeus essentially tells him to stop whining and says he'd throw Ares into Tartarus if he weren't his son.

Sparta honored Ares symbolically. They had a statue of him in chains, representing war bound by discipline. But the Spartans' real patron deities were Apollo and Artemis. Spartan warriors were elite because of discipline (Apollo's gift) and strategic thinking (Athena's domain), not mindless rage.

Hephaestus: The Divine Blacksmith's Revenge

We've mentioned Hephaestus already, but his own story deserves attention.

Hephaestus was either Zeus's son or Hera's son alone (she conceived him by herself in revenge for Zeus birthing Athena without her). Either way, he was deformed, possibly from birth or possibly from being thrown off Olympus.

In one story, Hera threw him off Olympus because he was ugly. He fell for a full day and landed in the ocean. The sea nymphs Thetis and Eurynome rescued him and raised him in a secret grotto beneath the sea.

There, he learned to work with metal, creating beautiful jewelry for his foster mothers.

Eventually, he sent Hera a beautiful golden throne as a gift. She sat in it, and magical chains sprang out, trapping her. No one could free her. Hephaestus refused to come back to Olympus and release her.

Finally, Dionysus got Hephaestus drunk and brought him back. Hephaestus freed Hera, but only after Zeus agreed to give him a place among the Olympians and arrange his marriage to Aphrodite.

Hephaestus's forge was said to be under volcanoes. When volcanoes erupted, it was because Hephaestus was working. He created Achilles's armor, Heracles's bronze clappers, Pandora (the first woman), and countless other wonders.

The gods needed him. He was the only one who could create the things they required. So they tolerated his presence, even if they didn't always respect him.

Hermes: The Trickster Messenger

Hermes was Zeus's son by the nymph Maia. He was the messenger of the gods, the god of travelers, thieves, commerce, and transitions. His symbol was the caduceus, a staff with two snakes wrapped around it.

Vulcan by Guillaume Coustou the Younger.'

Hermes was born in a cave. On his very first day, he climbed out of his cradle, found a tortoise, killed it, and used its shell to invent the lyre. Then he stole fifty cattle from Apollo's herd, cleverly making them walk backward so the tracks led in the wrong direction.

Apollo figured out who'd stolen his cattle and dragged baby Hermes before Zeus for judgment. Hermes lied convincingly. Zeus knew he was lying, but he was impressed by the newborn's cunning. He made Hermes return the cattle, but Hermes played his newly invented lyre so beautifully that Apollo traded the entire herd for the instrument.

This established Hermes's character. He was clever, quick, charming, and absolutely untrustworthy. He was, after all, the patron god of liars and thieves.

Hermes served as Zeus's messenger and carried out his orders. He led souls to the underworld. He helped heroes on quests. For example, he gave Perseus the sword to kill Medusa, helped Odysseus resist Circe's magic, and guided Heracles through various labors.

Hermes also had a dark side. He killed the hundred-eyed giant Argus on Zeus's orders. He also delivered Pandora to Epimetheus, knowing it would bring disaster to humanity.

But mostly, Hermes was likable. He was funny, helpful, and didn't take things too seriously. He represented the transition between states—between life and death, truth and lies, divine and mortal. He lived in the in-between spaces.

Dionysus: The God Who Died and Came Back

Dionysus is the strangest of the Olympians. He was the god of wine, ecstasy, theater, and madness. He died and was reborn. He was both Greek and foreign. He was male but often depicted as effeminate. He drove people insane but also brought divine joy. He was a contradiction wrapped in a mystery, soaked in wine.

His birth story is bizarre even by Greek standards. Zeus had an affair with Semele, a mortal princess of Thebes. When Semele became pregnant, Hera hatched a plan for revenge.

Hera disguised herself as an old woman and befriended Semele. She planted doubt in Semele's mind, saying, "How do you know your lover is really Zeus? He could be lying. If he truly loves you, he'll prove it by showing you his true divine form."

Semele, young and naive, asked Zeus to grant her one wish. Zeus was in love and swore by the River Styx—the most binding oath a god could make—that he would grant whatever she asked.

When Semele asked to see Zeus in his true form, Zeus knew it would kill her. But he'd sworn an oath. So, he revealed himself. The sight of Zeus in his full divine glory incinerated Semele instantly.

But their child survived. Zeus grabbed the unborn baby from Semele's ashes and sewed him into his thigh. Dionysus gestated there for three months, then was born a second time from Zeus's body. This made Dionysus "twice-born"—born once from his mother, once from his father.

Hera wasn't finished. She drove the infant Dionysus mad. Zeus sent him away to be raised by nymphs on Mount Nysa, far from Hera's reach. There, Dionysus discovered the grapevine and learned to make wine.

When Dionysus reached adulthood, he wandered the world teaching people viticulture (winemaking). He traveled to India, Egypt, and throughout Greece, always accompanied by his followers, the Maenads (frenzied female worshipers) and satyrs (half-man, half-goat creatures).

An oversized statue of Dionysus from the 2nd century CE.[10]

Dionysus's cult was ecstatic and wild. His followers danced themselves into trances, drank wine, and experienced divine madness. Women were especially drawn to his worship. The Maenads left their homes and families to roam the mountains, worshiping Dionysus in secret rites.

This terrified Greek men. A god who made women abandon domestic duties and act wild and free was very dangerous. Many kings and cities refused to recognize Dionysus as a god. This always ended badly for them.

King Pentheus of Thebes rejected Dionysus's divinity and tried to imprison him. Dionysus drove the women of Thebes, including Pentheus's own mother, into a Bacchic frenzy (Dionysus is known as Bacchus in Roman mythology). The women went to the mountains to worship. Pentheus dressed as a woman and went to spy on their rituals. The Maenads, in their madness, saw him as a wild animal. Led by his own mother, Agave, they tore Pentheus limb from limb with their bare hands. Agave carried her son's severed head back to Thebes as a trophy, only realizing what she'd done when the madness wore off.

King Lycurgus of Thrace attacked Dionysus and his followers. Dionysus drove Lycurgus mad in retaliation. In his insanity, Lycurgus killed his own son with an ax, thinking he was cutting down a grapevine. The land became barren until Lycurgus's own people executed him to appease Dionysus.

The pirates who kidnapped Dionysus (not knowing who he was) planned to sell him as a slave. Dionysus caused grapevines to grow all over their ship. He transformed into a lion, and phantom beasts appeared on deck. The terrified pirates jumped overboard. Dionysus turned them all into dolphins.

Eventually, all of Greece accepted him. Dionysus earned a place among the twelve Olympians, with Hestia graciously stepping aside to avoid conflict.

Dionysus also invented theater. His festivals in Athens featured dramatic competitions in which playwrights such as Aeschylus, Sophocles, and Euripides premiered their works. Greek tragedy and comedy both emerged from Dionysian worship. The theater mask—the symbol of drama—belonged to Dionysus.

Dionysus married Ariadne, the Cretan princess who helped Theseus defeat the Minotaur. While sailing home from Crete, Theseus abandoned Ariadne on the island of Naxos. Dionysus found her there, fell in love, and married her. He made her immortal and set her wedding crown among the stars as the constellation Corona Borealis.

Unlike most gods, Dionysus actually loved his wife and remained faithful to her. He also descended to the underworld and brought his mortal mother, Semele, back to life, making her a goddess. Dionysus had experienced mortality through his mother and rebirth through his unusual gestation. This made him uniquely sympathetic to human suffering.

Dionysus represented liberation from social constraints, rationality, and the ordinary world. Wine, theater, and ecstatic worship offered a temporary escape from the hardness of life. But Dionysus was also dangerous. Too much wine led to madness and violence. Too much liberation led to chaos. Dionysus offered both blessings and curses, often simultaneously.

The Greeks needed Dionysus. Apollo represented order, reason, and civilization. Dionysus represented disorder, emotion, and nature. Both were necessary. Too much Apollo made life rigid and cold. Too much Dionysus made life chaotic and destructive. Maintaining a balance between them was ideal but difficult.

The Olympian gods were a family, but they were not a happy one. They fought, cheated, loved, hated, and interfered in each other's lives constantly. They created most of their own problems. And those problems would spill over into the mortal world in countless myths.

But first, we need to talk about how humans came to exist in the first place. Because the gods didn't create humanity out of love or benevolence. They created humans by accident. And then they made humans' lives miserable on purpose.

Chapter 3: The Creation of "Us"

The gods had their domains. They had their palaces on Olympus. They had their power struggles and family drama. But something was missing: worshipers.

The gods didn't need humans to survive, but they demanded recognition. They wanted sacrifices, prayers, and temples. It was a contractual relationship. Humans provided ritual offerings, and the gods (in theory) maintained cosmic order and provided favorable conditions. Give us the smoke of burnt offerings, and we'll give you rain for your crops. Honor us, and we'll protect your city. Ignore us, and... well, you won't like what happens.

But humanity's creation wasn't exactly a carefully planned project. It felt more like something that went wrong from the start. And once humans existed, the gods spent considerable effort making their lives as difficult as possible.

Prometheus:
The Ultimate Rebel and the Theft of Fire

Prometheus was a Titan, but he was not like the others. He was the son of Iapetus, making him a cousin of Zeus rather than a sibling. His name meant "forethought." He could see the future and plan accordingly. His brother Epimetheus ("afterthought") could only understand things after they happened. This difference would doom them both.

During the Titanomachy, Prometheus sided with Zeus, as he knew Zeus would win. After the war, Zeus allowed Prometheus and his brother to remain free while most Titans rotted in Tartarus.

The gods decided to create mortal creatures to populate the earth. They assigned the task to Prometheus and Epimetheus. Here's where things went wrong. Epimetheus, living up to his name, gave out gifts to the animals without thinking ahead. He gave strength to the lions, speed to the deer, flight to the birds, thick fur to the bears, sharp claws to the wolves, and shells to the turtles. By the time he got to humans, he'd given away all the good survival traits. Humans were left naked, slow, weak, and vulnerable. They were basically defenseless.

Prometheus had to fix his brother's mistake. Humans needed something special to survive. That's when he turned his attention to the gods' exclusive possession: fire.

The first conflict came during a sacrifice at Mecone. Prometheus was mediating between the gods and humans, establishing how sacrifices would work. He slaughtered an ox and divided it into two portions, letting Zeus choose which portion the gods would receive from future sacrifices.

Prometheus wrapped the good meat in the ox's stomach—unappetizing but valuable. He wrapped the bones in a thick layer of glistening fat—attractive but worthless.

Zeus chose the fat-wrapped bones. Some sources say he was fooled. Others say he knew exactly what Prometheus was doing but chose the worst portion anyway, wanting an excuse to punish humanity.

Zeus was furious either way. As punishment, he denied humanity the use of fire. Without fire, humans couldn't cook food, forge tools, or keep warm. They would remain primitive and helpless.

Prometheus couldn't accept this. Fire represented civilization, technology, and progress—everything that could raise humans above mere survival. So, he committed an act of rebellion that would echo through eternity.

Prometheus snuck into Olympus. He went to the forge of Hephaestus (or to the chariot of the sun god Helios, depending on the version) and stole fire. He carried it down to earth in a hollow fennel stalk, which could smolder for hours without burning through.

He stole fire and gave it to humanity.

With fire, humans could cook meat, forge tools, warm themselves in winter, and light the darkness. Fire made civilization possible.

But Prometheus gave more than just fire. He taught humanity mathematics, astronomy, and how to read the stars and predict seasons. He taught them medicine, architecture, animal husbandry, and even writing. He transformed humans from vulnerable animals into something capable of civilization. This is why Zeus's fury was so intense.

Zeus's punishment was creative and eternal. He had Prometheus chained to a rock in the Caucasus Mountains. Every day, an eagle would fly to Prometheus and eat his liver. Every night, because Prometheus was immortal, his liver would regenerate. The next day, the eagle would return and eat it again.

This torture continued for hundreds, maybe thousands of years. Prometheus endured it all, never apologizing and never begging for mercy. He knew the future, so he knew he would eventually be freed, but not when or how.

The Torture of Prometheus *by Salvator Rosa.*[11]

Prometheus also knew a dangerous secret. He knew which woman would bear the son prophesied to overthrow Zeus. He refused to reveal this information even under torture, for it was his only leverage. Eventually, he traded the secret for his freedom. The sea nymph Thetis would lead to his downfall. Zeus, who'd been pursuing Thetis, immediately arranged for her to marry a mortal instead.

Eventually, the hero Heracles, during his labors, came upon Prometheus and killed the eagle. Zeus allowed this because Heracles was his son, and it added to his son's glory. But Zeus required something in exchange. Prometheus had to wear a ring made from his chains, set with a piece of the stone he'd been bound to, as a reminder of his punishment.

Prometheus's suffering was meant as a warning. Defy the gods, and even immortality won't save you from regret. But Prometheus became something else entirely—the rebel who suffers for helping humanity, who brings progress despite divine opposition, and who chooses mortal welfare over divine authority.

The Greeks never quite knew what to make of him. Was he a hero or a cautionary tale? Both, probably. But humanity had fire, and that changed everything.

Pandora's Box:

The Greek "Eve" and the Origin of Human Suffering

Zeus wasn't finished punishing humanity for receiving stolen fire. He decided to send them a gift that would curse them forever.

He ordered Hephaestus to create the first woman.

Up until this point, according to Hesiod, only men existed. They lived simple lives, working the earth and dying peacefully. However, Zeus wanted to introduce something that would make their lives more difficult.

Hephaestus shaped a woman from clay and water, creating a form of stunning beauty. Each god contributed something to her creation. Athena taught her to weave and dressed her in fine clothes. Aphrodite gave her irresistible beauty and desire. Hermes gave her a deceitful nature and the ability to lie convincingly. The Graces (the goddesses who personify grace and beauty) and Horae (the goddesses of the seasons and the passage of time) adorned her with jewelry and flowers.

They named her Pandora, meaning "all-gifted," because all the gods had given her gifts. But these weren't blessings. They were weapons.

Zeus sent Pandora to Epimetheus, Prometheus's brother. Prometheus had warned Epimetheus beforehand. "Never accept gifts from Zeus. It's a trap." But Epimetheus, true to his name ("afterthought"), only understood things after they happened. He saw Pandora's beauty and ignored his brother's warning. He accepted her as his wife.

Pandora came with a jar, not a box—that's a mistranslation from the Renaissance. The Greek word is *pithos*, a large storage jar. Zeus or Hermes gave it to her with specific instructions to never open it.

Of course, this was the trap. You don't tell someone to never open something unless you want them to do exactly that.

Pandora had been created with curiosity and deceit as part of her nature. As time passed, the thought of what was inside the jar became too much to resist. She opened the jar.

Out flew every evil that would plague humanity: sickness, death, toil, pain, sorrow, despair, greed, violence, jealousy—every form of suffering. They spread across the world like a dark cloud. Humans, who had lived relatively peaceful lives until then, were suddenly cursed with misery.

Pandora slammed the lid shut, but it was too late. Everything had escaped.

Except for one thing.

At the bottom of the jar remained Elpis—Hope.

Why was Hope trapped in a jar of evils? The Greeks debated this. Some said Hope was left for humanity to cling to when everything else was terrible. Others said Hope was actually an evil too—false hope keeps people suffering instead of giving up. The ambiguity was probably intentional. Hope could be either comfort or delusion, depending on the circumstance.

The Pandora myth explained why life was hard. Why do we get sick, have to work, and deal with lies and violence? Because Pandora opened the jar.

It also reflected Greek attitudes toward women. Hesiod presents Pandora as a "beautiful evil," created specifically to punish men, with a "shameless mind and deceitful nature." Women were dangerous—beautiful on the outside, treacherous within. The myth helped justify keeping women powerless. If the first woman brought all evil into the world, then obviously, women needed to be controlled.

But there's another reading that complicates this. Pandora was created by Zeus as a weapon, but she was still a victim. She was made to be curious and then punished for acting on her nature. She was made beautiful and then blamed for being desirable. The gods created her to cause suffering and then blamed her for it. She had no choice in her creation, no say in her nature, and no chance to refuse her purpose. She was, in every sense, a tool used by the gods to hurt humanity.

This reading makes Pandora tragic rather than villainous. She was humanity's first victim, not its first criminal.

The pattern should sound familiar too: a woman is created, given instructions that set her up to fail, disobeys, and brings suffering to all humanity. The Garden of Eden story follows the same structure. In both myths, women are blamed for why life is hard.

But the Greeks never claimed humans were meant to live in paradise. They didn't promise future redemption or heaven. The Pandora myth just explained why life was hard, not that it would get better. You lived, you suffered, and you died. Hope might make it bearable, but it didn't change reality.

Pandora and Epimetheus had a daughter, Pyrrha, who would marry Deucalion (Prometheus's son). This brings us to another crucial myth that Hesiod mentions but other sources tell more completely: the Great Flood.

Zeus, disgusted by human wickedness during the Bronze Age (or possibly the Iron Age—sources vary), decided to destroy humanity. He sent a catastrophic flood that covered the earth. For nine days and nine nights, rain poured from the sky while Poseidon's earthquakes shattered the land. Mountains disappeared under water. Cities were swallowed. Every human drowned.

Except for two.

Prometheus, able to see the future, warned his son Deucalion about the coming flood. Deucalion built a wooden chest (a boat in some versions) and climbed inside with his wife, Pyrrha. They floated for nine days until the waters receded and their vessel came to rest on Mount Parnassus (or Mount Othrys).

When they emerged, they were alone. The entire human race had been wiped out. They went to the Oracle at Delphi (which somehow survived the flood) and asked what to do. The Oracle told them, "Veil your heads and throw the bones of your mother behind you."

This seemed like a terrible instruction. Desecrating their mother's bones would be incredibly impious. But Deucalion realized the Oracle meant their mother, Gaia, the Earth. The bones of the earth were stones.

They veiled their heads, walked forward, and threw stones over their shoulders. The stones Deucalion threw became men. The stones Pyrrha threw became women. Slowly, humanity was reborn, literally from the earth, just as Prometheus had originally created humans from clay.

This flood myth shares obvious parallels with the biblical flood story and other Near Eastern flood myths, particularly the *Epic of Gilgamesh* from Mesopotamia. Whether the Greeks borrowed the story, shared a common source, or developed it independently, the flood represented a cosmic reset. It was Zeus's attempt to start over with humanity.

But Zeus didn't create better humans. The stones became people who were no less flawed than before. The flood solved nothing. Humans remained humans. They were capable of both good and evil, but mostly they were just trying to survive in a world that didn't care about them.

So, in a way, all humans after the flood are descended from Pandora through Pyrrha. We all carry the legacy of that opened jar. Every evil that escaped still plagues us. Hope still remains. However, even that might be a curse.

The Five Ages of Man: From the Golden Age to the Iron Age (Where We Are Now)

Hesiod, in his *Works and Days*, describes human history as five successive ages, each worse than the last. This wasn't evolution or progress. It was actually a decline. Humans started great and became progressively worse.

The Golden Age

The first humans lived during Cronus's reign, before Zeus took power. These were the men of gold. They lived like gods. They had no work or sorrow. They did not grow old. The earth produced food spontaneously. They spent their days feasting and enjoying life. When death came, it was like falling asleep. They felt no pain.

After they died, Zeus honored them. They became spirits who wandered the earth, watching over and protecting living humans. They were invisible guardians, rewarding good and punishing evil.

This was paradise. It didn't last.

The Silver Age

Zeus created the second race of humans, the men of silver. They were far inferior to the men of gold. They remained children for a hundred years, cared for by their mothers. When they finally reached adulthood, they lived only a short time because they were foolish and violent. They refused to honor the gods or make sacrifices.

Zeus destroyed them for their impiety. But he allowed them some honor. After death, they became "blessed spirits of the underworld." They had some status, but nothing like the golden race.

The silver age was already a step down. Humans were more childish, more violent, and less pious. The decline had begun.

The Bronze Age

Zeus created a third race, the men of bronze. They were completely different from the silver race. They were obsessed with violence and war. They had bronze weapons, bronze armor, and bronze houses. They ate meat and fought constantly.

But they weren't warriors in any noble sense. They were brutal and savage. They destroyed each other through endless warfare. No one killed them. They killed themselves. When they died, they went to Hades without any special honor. They were forgotten.

The bronze age represented war without honor, violence without purpose. Strength without wisdom destroys itself.

The Age of Heroes

Here's where Hesiod breaks his pattern. Instead of continuing the decline, he inserts a fourth age that's actually better than the third: the age of heroes.

This was the time of the demigods. Zeus fathered children with mortal women, and those children became heroes. Heracles, Perseus, Theseus, and Achilles were born in this age. They were more just and noble than the bronze race, though they were still violent.

Many died in battle, but Zeus honored them. He sent some to the Elysian Fields, a paradise at the edge of the world where they lived in eternal happiness. Others became spirits that mortals could appeal to for help.

This age was Hesiod's own past, the time of the great epics and legends. It was better than what came before and after. But it still ended.

The Iron Age

Finally, the fifth and current age is the iron age. Hesiod describes it as the worst of all.

Humans of the iron age must work hard for everything. Parents and children have no natural love for each other. Friends betray friends. Hospitality and honor mean nothing. Might makes right. Justice is decided by force and fraud.

Hesiod goes into painful detail about the iron age. Brother will fight brother. Children will dishonor their aging parents, refusing to care for them and criticizing them harshly. Oaths mean nothing.

Good people suffer while evil people prosper. No one feels shame for wrongdoing. Eventually, Aidos (Shame) and Nemesis (Righteous Anger) will abandon humanity entirely, leaving to join the gods on Olympus, their beautiful forms wrapped in white robes as they depart. When that happens, humans will have no defense against complete moral collapse. Only suffering will remain, and there will be no remedy.

Hesiod was writing around 700 BCE, and he already thought the world had gone to hell. He looked at farmers struggling with debt, nobles abusing power, and traditional values crumbling and concluded everything was worse than it used to be.

Every generation thinks this. The "golden age" is always the past. The current age is always the worst.

The five ages also explained why life was difficult without entirely blaming humans. The decline wasn't just humanity's fault. It was cosmic. The universe itself was degrading, like metal corrupting from gold to iron. Hesiod lived when iron tools replaced bronze ones, and older generations remembered bronze as the time of greater heroes. The technological shift became a metaphor for moral decline.

This was deeply pessimistic. No redemption was coming. There would be no savior. No return to the golden age. The Fates had already measured your thread. The universe was indifferent to your happiness. You would suffer regardless.

Yet people kept living. They farmed, raised children, built cities, and created art. They knew life was hard and unfair, but they lived anyway. Hope kept people moving forward.

Chapter 4: The Twelve Labors and the Heavy Hitters

The gods created a flawed world and populated it with suffering humans. But from this mess emerged something unexpected: heroes.

Greek heroes weren't perfect. They lied, cheated, murdered, and abandoned people who trusted them. But they also accomplished extraordinary feats and killed unkillable monsters, showing that even weak mortals could achieve greatness.

The greatest heroes were almost always demigods, the children of gods and mortals. They inherited some divine power but remained mortal and vulnerable. They could be wounded, tricked, and killed. This made their achievements meaningful. When a god slays a monster, that's expected. When a half-mortal human does it while bleeding and exhausted, that's heroic.

Heracles (Hercules):
The Twelve Labors and the Price of Strength

Heracles (the Romans called him Hercules, which is the name most people know) was the greatest hero in Greek mythology. He was the strongest man who ever lived. He killed monsters that terrified gods. He performed twelve impossible labors and survived.

But his story isn't triumphant. It's tragic. Heracles was a weapon that destroyed everyone around him, including himself.

The Birth and Hera's Hatred

Heracles was Zeus's son by Alcmene, a mortal woman. Zeus disguised himself as Alcmene's husband, Amphitryon, who was away at war, and slept with her. Later that same night, the real Amphitryon came home and also slept with his wife. Alcmene became pregnant with twins: Heracles, son of Zeus, and Iphicles, son of Amphitryon.

Zeus, proud of his half-mortal son, boasted that a descendant of Perseus born that day would rule all of Greece. Hera, enraged by yet another of Zeus's affairs, delayed Heracles's birth and accelerated the birth of another Perseus descendant, Eurystheus. When Eurystheus was born first, he became the rightful king. Zeus couldn't break his own oath. Heracles would serve Eurystheus, not rule him.

Hera tried to kill Heracles in his cradle. She sent two massive serpents to strangle the infant. But baby Heracles grabbed the snakes and strangled them with his bare hands. His strength was already superhuman.

Hera's hatred would pursue Heracles his entire life. She couldn't kill him, as Zeus protected his son, but she could make his life miserable. And she certainly did.

One of the most famous depictions of Heracles.[12]

The Madness and the Crime

Heracles grew up strong, brave, and skilled. He married Megara, princess of Thebes, and they had children. For a while, he was happy.

Then Hera struck. She drove Heracles mad. In his madness, he didn't recognize his own family. He saw enemies everywhere. In a fit of insane rage, he killed Megara and their children.

When the madness lifted and Heracles realized what he'd done, he was devastated. He wanted to die. However, suicide was considered cowardly in Greek culture. Instead, he went to the Oracle at Delphi to ask how he could atone.

The Oracle told him to serve King Eurystheus of Mycenae for twelve years and perform whatever labors Eurystheus demanded. If he succeeded, he would be purified of his crime and granted immortality.

Eurystheus, remembering the prophecy that Heracles should have ruled instead, hated Heracles and wanted him dead. So, he said the hero had to complete ten tasks, each intended to harm or kill him. (There would ultimately be twelve tasks; Eurystheus decided that two of them didn't count.)

Heracles completed them all.

The Twelve Labors

Labor 1: The Nemean Lion

Heracles was ordered to kill a lion terrorizing Nemea. This sounds simple enough, except this lion's hide was impervious to weapons. Arrows bounced off it. Swords broke. Spears shattered.

Heracles tracked the lion to its cave, which had two entrances. He blocked one, entered through the other, and strangled the beast with his bare hands.

No blade could cut the hide, so he used the lion's own claws to skin it. From then on, Heracles wore the Nemean Lion's skin as armor and its head as a helmet.

Labor 2: The Lernaean Hydra

The Hydra lived in the swamps of Lerna. It was a serpent-like monster with multiple heads and poisonous breath. Worse, if you cut off one head, two grew back.

Heracles brought his nephew Iolaus. He attacked, cutting off heads, but they kept growing back. This was going to be an endless battle.

Iolaus had an idea. They should cauterize the neck stumps with fire immediately after cutting the head off. It worked. The two systematically destroyed all the heads except the immortal central one, which Heracles buried under a massive rock.

Heracles dipped his arrows in the Hydra's poisonous blood, making them lethal. These arrows would later cause his own death.

Eurystheus declared that this labor didn't count because Heracles had help.

Labor 3: The Ceryneian Hind

Next, Heracles had to capture Artemis's sacred golden-horned hind alive. Killing it would bring divine wrath. Catching it without harm seemed impossible.

Heracles pursued it for an entire year across Greece and beyond. The chase tested his endurance, not his strength. Finally, through patience rather than force, he captured it and carried it back to Mycenae.

Artemis confronted him, furious. He explained he was following the Oracle's orders. She accepted this, although she was still upset, and took her hind back.

Labor 4: The Erymanthian Boar

Heracles had to capture a massive wild boar terrorizing Mount Erymanthos. Alive.

On the way, Heracles visited Pholus, a civilized centaur. They opened the wine belonging to all the centaurs. The smell drove the wild centaurs into a frenzy, and they attacked.

Heracles fought them off with his Hydra-poisoned arrows. He accidentally hit Pholus and Chiron, the wise centaur who'd trained many heroes. Both were immortal, so the poison couldn't kill them, but it caused eternal agony. Chiron would later give up his immortality to escape the pain.

Heracles reached the boar, chased it into deep snow, and captured it. Eurystheus was so terrified that he hid in a buried jar.

Labor 5: The Augean Stables

The fifth labor was not dangerous, but it was demeaning. Heracles was ordered to clean the stables of King Augeas, who owned the largest herd of cattle in Greece. The stables hadn't been cleaned in thirty years. The stench carried for miles.

Eurystheus chose this labor to humiliate Heracles, forcing a mighty demigod to shovel dung like a common servant. But Heracles outwitted them all.

He offered Augeas a deal. If he cleaned the stables in a single day, he would be paid a tenth of the cattle. Augeas agreed, laughing, certain it couldn't be done.

Heracles tore holes in the stable walls and diverted the Alpheios and Peneios Rivers through them. The rushing water blasted away all the filth in mere hours. The stables were spotless.

Augeas, furious at being tricked, refused to pay. He claimed Heracles had acted on Eurystheus's orders and took no risk. Heracles sued him in court. When Augeas's son Phyleus testified in Heracles's favor, Augeas banished them both.

Eurystheus then disqualified the labor, saying Heracles had tried to profit from it.

Labor 6: The Stymphalian Birds

The Stymphalian Birds were man-eating birds with bronze beaks. They lived around Lake Stymphalos and could shoot their metallic feathers like arrows. Eurystheus wanted Heracles to drive them away.

Athena gave Heracles bronze castanets made by Hephaestus. He climbed a mountain and clashed them together. The noise startled the birds into flight, which allowed him to shoot them down with arrows. The survivors fled.

Labor 7: The Cretan Bull

The seventh labor was to capture the Cretan Bull alive. This was no ordinary beast. It had been sent by Poseidon to King Minos of Crete as a sign of favor. It was meant to be sacrificed. But Minos, taken by the bull's beauty, refused. To punish him, Poseidon drove the bull mad, and it began rampaging across Crete, destroying farmland and terrifying the island.

Heracles sailed to Crete and asked Minos for permission to take the bull. Minos agreed, glad to be rid of it. Heracles tracked the beast across the countryside. When it charged, he met it head-on, grabbed its horns, and wrestled it into submission.

He brought it back to Mycenae. Eurystheus, horrified, tried to offer it as a sacrifice to Hera, but she refused to accept anything touched by Heracles. The bull was released and wandered east, eventually reaching Marathon, where it would later be slain by Theseus.

Labor 8: The Mares of Diomedes

Next, Heracles had to capture the man-eating mares of Diomedes, a Thracian king and son of Ares. These horses were no ordinary animals. They were trained to feast on human flesh, kept savage by a constant diet of strangers, prisoners, and enemies. Diomedes ruled by fear, feeding his victims to the beasts to show his power.

Heracles arrived with a small band of companions and stole the mares from their stables. Diomedes and his warriors gave chase. In the chaos, Heracles left Abderus, a young man often described as his lover or squire, to guard the horses. But the mares turned on Abderus and tore him apart.

Heracles returned too late. Grief-stricken and enraged, he killed Diomedes and, in some versions, fed the king's body to the very horses he had raised on human flesh. The mares, calmed by the death of their master, grew docile.

Heracles brought them to Eurystheus, who released them into the wild. Some say they wandered as far as Mount Olympus, where they were eventually killed by wild animals.

In memory of Abderus, Heracles later founded the city of Abdera near the site where the boy died.

Labor 9: The Belt of Hippolyta

The ninth labor was to retrieve the belt of Hippolyta, queen of the Amazons. The belt was a gift from Ares and became a symbol of her authority, strength, and divine favor. Eurystheus demanded it for his daughter.

Heracles expected a hard fight. The Amazons were legendary warriors. They had been trained from childhood and lived in a society ruled by women and shaped by war. But to his surprise, Hippolyta welcomed him peacefully. She admired his strength and valor and willingly agreed to give him the belt.

For once, no violence was needed. The labor could have ended with respect and diplomacy.

But Hera, still scheming against Heracles, disguised herself as an Amazon and spread a rumor that Heracles planned to abduct Hippolyta. The Amazons, believing their queen was in danger, attacked Heracles's camp.

In the chaos, Heracles believed Hippolyta had betrayed him. He killed her and took the belt. Only later did he learn that she had meant to help him and that the battle had been manufactured by Hera's lies.

Labor 10: The Cattle of Geryon

The tenth labor was to steal the cattle of Geryon, a fearsome three-bodied Giant who lived on the distant island of Erytheia, beyond the western edge of the world. The cattle were guarded by Orthrus, a two-headed dog, and Eurytion, a Giant herdsman.

Heracles began the long journey west, traveling across North Africa. The desert heat was so unbearable that he shot an arrow at the sun. Rather than strike him down, Helios, the sun god, admired his boldness and loaned him a golden cup. This vessel could carry Heracles across the sea to Erytheia.

On the island, Heracles was met by Orthrus, whom he killed with his club. He then killed Eurytion and finally faced Geryon. Heracles shot a Hydra-poisoned arrow that pierced all three torsos, killing him instantly.

Herding the cattle back to Greece was no easy feat. Hera sent gadflies to scatter them, and in Italy, a fire-breathing Giant named Cacus stole part of the herd and hid them in a cave. Heracles strangled him and reclaimed the cattle.

At last, he returned to Eurystheus, who accepted the cattle and sacrificed them to Hera, perhaps out of fear or spite.

Labor 11: The Apples of the Hesperides

Next, Heracles had to retrieve the golden apples of the Hesperides, sacred fruits that grew in a secret garden at the edge of the world. These apples were a wedding gift from Gaia to Hera and were said to grant immortality. They were guarded by the Hesperides, nymphs of the evening, and Ladon, a monstrous, hundred-headed dragon who never slept.

No mortal knew where the garden was. Heracles wandered the edges of the earth, seeking its location. Eventually, he found the ancient sea god Nereus, who knew all things but would not speak easily. When Heracles tried to question him, Nereus transformed into water, fire, beasts, and shadow. Heracles held on through every change until Nereus gave in and told him where to go.

Heracles found the garden, but he could not enter. So, he sought out Atlas, the Titan condemned to hold up the sky as punishment for rebelling against the gods. Heracles offered him a deal. He would bear the sky if Atlas would fetch the apples.

Atlas, desperate for relief, agreed. He returned with the apples but then refused to take back the burden of the sky. Heracles, thinking fast, tricked him. He asked Atlas to hold the sky just for a moment while he adjusted his cloak. Atlas agreed. Heracles took the apples and left while the Titan roared at him to come back.

He returned the apples to Eurystheus, who handed them to Hera. But since they were sacred to her, she returned them to the garden.

Labor 12: Cerberus

The final labor was the most dangerous. Heracles had to descend into the underworld, capture Cerberus—the monstrous three-headed hound of Hades—and bring him back to the world of the living.

Before he could begin, Heracles was initiated into the Eleusinian Mysteries, the secret rites of Demeter and Persephone. These rituals revealed to him how to enter the land of the dead without perishing and, more importantly, how to return.

He descended into the underworld, crossing rivers of fire and sorrow, walking among the souls of the dead, past kings and criminals, judges and phantoms. Even in Hades, his legend preceded him.

Heracles approached Hades and Persephone and asked for permission to take Cerberus. Hades agreed, but only if Heracles could subdue the beast without using weapons.

Cerberus met him at the gates. Its three heads snarled at him, fangs dripping with venom. It had a serpent for a tail and a body muscled with divine rage. The beast lunged, but Heracles grappled it barehanded, enduring bites, scratches, and tail lashes. At last, he choked the monster into submission and dragged it up to the surface.

When Eurystheus saw Heracles leading Cerberus through the gates of Mycenae, he was so terrified that he hid in a bronze jar, trembling.

Heracles returned Cerberus to the underworld, keeping his promise to Hades. The labors were finished. His crime was atoned for, and his name had been immortalized. He had done what no mortal was ever meant to do: he entered the realm of death and came back victorious.

A mosaic of all Twelve Labors.[18]

After the Labors

Completing the labors didn't end Heracles's troubles. He went on to have many more adventures, most of which ended in tragedy.

Remember how Augeas refused to pay Heracles for cleaning the stables? Heracles didn't forget. After his labors were complete, he raised an army and marched on Elis. He killed Augeas and his other sons, placing Phyleus on the throne. During this campaign, Heracles is said to have founded the Olympic Games at Olympia.

This wasn't the only time Heracles sought revenge. The Trojan king Laomedon promised Heracles divine horses if he would rescue his daughter Hesione from a sea monster. Poseidon had sent it to punish Laomedon for not paying him and Apollo for building Troy's walls. Heracles killed the monster, but Laomedon refused to pay him. Heracles vowed revenge and later returned with an army. He sacked Troy, killed Laomedon and most of his sons, and gave Hesione to his ally Telamon. Only the young prince Priam survived. Priam would later be king during the more famous Trojan War.

Heracles was so powerful that he even wounded gods, something almost no other mortal achieved. He shot Hera with an arrow, causing her divine blood to flow. He wounded Ares with an arrow, forcing even the god of war to flee to Olympus in pain. He even wounded Hades when the lord of the underworld came to the surface to fight at Pylos. Even Olympians could bleed when facing Heracles.

Years after his labors, Heracles competed for the hand of Deianira, princess of Calydon. He had to wrestle the river god Achelous, who transformed into various forms, including a bull, a serpent, and a bull-headed man. Heracles defeated him in each form and won Deianira as his bride.

Later, when Heracles and Deianira were traveling, they came to the River Evenus, which was flooded. The centaur Nessus, who worked there as a ferryman, offered to carry Deianira across while Heracles swam. But halfway across, Nessus tried to rape her. From the opposite bank, Heracles shot him with one of his Hydra-poisoned arrows.

As Nessus died, he told Deianira to collect his blood, claiming it was a love potion that would keep Heracles faithful. Deianira believed him and kept the blood for years.

Years passed. Heracles captured a city and brought home a beautiful young woman, Iole, as a prize. Deianira feared that Heracles loved Iole, so she sent him a robe soaked in Nessus's blood (the "love potion").

It wasn't a love potion. It was Hydra poison. When Heracles put on the robe, the poison burned into his skin. He couldn't remove the robe, as it had fused to his flesh. The pain was unbearable.

Heracles knew he was dying. He built a funeral pyre on Mount Oeta and ordered it lit. As the flames consumed him, Zeus took pity on his son. He brought Heracles to Olympus and made him immortal. Heracles married Hebe, the goddess of youth, and finally reconciled with Hera.

Heracles's story is brutal. Strength couldn't save him from Hera's hatred, his own madness, or the consequences of his actions. His life was defined by violence he couldn't control. Even his death came from trying to help someone.

But despite everything, he completed every impossible task. He survived every monster. And in the end, he achieved what few mortals ever did: he gained immortality.

Perseus:
Medusa, the Kraken, and the First "Superhero" Arc

If Perseus lived today, he'd have a movie franchise. He follows what we'd now call the classic superhero origin story. He had divine parentage, cool gadgets from mentors, and an impossible quest. He saved the girl, defeated the monster, and became a king. The Greeks didn't call it a "superhero arc," but they invented the pattern 2,500 years before comic books existed.

The Prophecy and the Bronze Chamber

King Acrisius of Argos received a prophecy. His daughter, Danaë, would bear a son who would kill him. To prevent this, Acrisius locked Danaë in a bronze chamber underground, making sure no man could reach her.

Zeus, however, didn't need doors. He transformed into a shower of golden light or golden rain, depending on the version, and entered the chamber. He impregnated Danaë, and nine months later, she gave birth to Perseus.

When Acrisius discovered the baby, he refused to kill his own daughter and grandson directly. That would anger the gods. Instead, he sealed them in a wooden chest and threw it into the sea. If they died, the sea would be to blame, not him.

The chest drifted and eventually washed ashore on the island of Seriphos. A fisherman named Dictys found it and took in Danaë and Perseus.

The Impossible Task

Perseus grew up on Seriphos. When he reached adulthood, the king of the island, Polydectes, fell in love with Danaë. She rejected him. Polydectes decided to get rid of Perseus so he could pressure Danaë without interference.

Polydectes announced he was courting another woman and demanded wedding gifts from everyone. Perseus was poor and had nothing to give, so he rashly promised he would bring back the head of Medusa, one of the three Gorgons.

Polydectes seized the chance to get rid of Perseus. The Gorgons were monsters with snakes for hair and faces so hideous that anyone who looked at them turned instantly to stone. Medusa was the only mortal

Gorgon, which meant she could be killed, theoretically. But no one had ever succeeded.

Perseus would have died if not for divine help.

The Divine Arsenal

Athena and Hermes decided to help Perseus. Athena had her own grudge against Medusa. Medusa had once been a beautiful woman, but Poseidon raped her in Athena's temple. Instead of punishing Poseidon, Athena punished Medusa, transforming her into a monster. Now, Athena wanted Medusa dead, and Perseus was her weapon.

The gods sent Perseus on a quest to gather magical items. First, he had to find the Graeae, three ancient women who shared a single eye and a single tooth. They knew where to find the items Perseus needed.

Perseus snuck up on the Graeae and stole their eye while they were passing it between them. Blind and helpless, they told him where to find the nymphs who possessed the magical gear.

The nymphs gave Perseus winged sandals, so he could fly; a *kibisis*, a magical bag that could safely hold Medusa's head, and the Cap of Invisibility, Hades's helmet.

Athena also gave him a polished bronze shield that could serve as a mirror. Hermes gave him an adamantine sword that could cut through anything.

Slaying Medusa

Perseus flew to the lair of the Gorgons. The three sisters, Stheno, Euryale, and Medusa, were sleeping. Perseus used Athena's shield as a mirror so he could see Medusa without looking at her directly. He approached her while invisible, guided by the reflection.

In one clean stroke, he cut off Medusa's head. From her neck sprang two offspring: Pegasus, the winged horse, and Chrysaor, a Giant with a golden sword. Both were Poseidon's children; they had been conceived when he raped Medusa before her transformation.

Perseus stuffed Medusa's head into the *kibisis* and flew away. The other two Gorgons woke and pursued him, but he was invisible and escaped.

Saving Andromeda

On his way home, Perseus flew over Ethiopia. The Greeks called any land south of Egypt "Ethiopia." He saw a beautiful woman chained to a rock by the sea, apparently being offered as a sacrifice.

This was Andromeda. Her mother, Queen Cassiopeia, had boasted that Andromeda was more beautiful than the Nereids, the sea nymphs. The Nereids complained to Poseidon, who sent a sea monster, Cetus, to ravage the coast. The Greeks described it as a sea monster or a large whale. Modern people would call it the Kraken, but that is actually a Norse monster from Scandinavian legends that came about two thousand years later.

An oracle said the only way to appease Poseidon was to sacrifice Andromeda to Cetus. King Cepheus and Cassiopeia, desperate to save their kingdom, chained their daughter to a rock.

Perseus arrived just as Cetus emerged from the sea. He swooped down, showed the monster Medusa's head, and turned it to stone. He freed Andromeda and claimed her as his bride.

Perseus and Andromeda *by Titian.*[14]

There was a complication, though. Andromeda had been engaged to her uncle Phineus. At the wedding feast, Phineus and his supporters attacked, trying to take Andromeda back by force. Perseus was outnumbered. He was forced to pull out Medusa's head, turning all his attackers to stone.

The Prophecy Fulfilled

Perseus returned to Seriphos with Andromeda and found that Polydectes was still harassing Danaë. Perseus crashed the king's banquet and revealed Medusa's head, turning Polydectes and all his supporters to stone. He made Dictys, the kind fisherman who had rescued him, the new king.

Perseus gave Medusa's head to Athena, who mounted it on her shield, the aegis, where it remained forever.

Finally, Perseus returned to Argos to meet his grandfather, Acrisius. But Acrisius, remembering the prophecy, fled. Perseus pursued him, not to kill him but to convince him there was no danger.

At athletic games in Larissa, Perseus competed in the discus throw. His throw went wide. He struck an old man in the crowd, killing him. The old man was Acrisius, who had fled to Larissa. The prophecy was fulfilled through accident, not intent.

Perseus, ashamed to rule Argos after killing its king—even accidentally—exchanged kingdoms with the king of Tiryns. He founded the city of Mycenae, which would become one of the most powerful cities in Greece. The massive walls of Mycenae, built with stones so large that later Greeks believed only the Cyclopes could have moved them, were called "Cyclopean walls."

Perseus and Andromeda had many children. Their descendants included some of the most important figures in Greek mythology. Perseus's grandson was Amphitryon, the mortal father of Heracles.

Unlike many Greek heroes, Perseus did not die in battle, exile, or madness. He is said to have died peacefully, either in Mycenae or another part of his kingdom. After his death, the gods placed him among the stars as the constellation Perseus, alongside Andromeda and Pegasus.

Perseus's story established patterns that would repeat throughout Greek mythology. Divine parentage gives you advantages but also attracts divine hatred. Prophecies will be fulfilled no matter how hard you try to prevent them. Magic items and divine help can get you through impossible situations, but they don't guarantee happiness. You can defeat monsters and save princesses, but you can't escape fate.

Theseus: The Minotaur, the Labyrinth, and the Founding of Athens

Theseus was Athens's greatest hero, their answer to Sparta's claims of superior warriors and Thebes's legendary founders. Athens needed a hero who embodied intelligence, courage, and political savvy. The Athenians created Theseus.

His myth is partly propaganda. Athens was a major power by the 5th century BCE, and it retrofitted its history with a legendary founder who could match anyone else's heroes. But the story, propaganda or not, became one of the most famous in Greek mythology.

His Birth and the Sandals

Theseus had two fathers, a uniquely Greek concept called dual paternity. His mother, Aethra, slept with King Aegeus of Athens one night, and later that same night, she slept with Poseidon, god of the sea. Theseus was both a mortal prince, inheriting the throne through Aegeus, and a demigod, inheriting supernatural strength from Poseidon.

Before leaving, Aegeus hid his sword and sandals under a massive boulder. He told Aethra that when the boy was strong enough to lift the boulder and retrieve these items, she should send him to Athens. That would prove he was worthy to be acknowledged as his heir.

Theseus grew up in Troezen, raised by his mother and grandfather. When he came of age, he easily lifted the boulder and claimed the sword and sandals. His grandfather wanted him to sail safely to Athens, but Theseus chose the dangerous land route because he wanted to prove himself through heroic deeds.

The Journey to Athens

Along the road to Athens, Theseus encountered six villains who terrorized travelers. He killed them all using their own methods. It was truly poetic justice.

Periphetes the Club-bearer attacked travelers with a bronze club. Theseus killed him and took the club as his weapon.

Sinis the Pine-Bender bent pine trees to the ground and tied victims to them. When he released the trees, they would spring back up, tearing the victim apart. Theseus killed him the same way.

The Crommyonian Sow was a giant, murderous pig. Theseus hunted and killed it.

Sciron forced travelers to wash his feet at a cliff edge and then kicked them off to be eaten by a giant turtle below. Theseus kicked Sciron off the cliff instead.

Cercyon challenged travelers to wrestling matches and killed the losers. Theseus wrestled him and broke his back.

Procrustes offered travelers hospitality but forced them onto an iron bed. If they were too short, he stretched them on a rack. If they were too tall, he cut off their legs to make them fit. Theseus killed him by making him fit his own bed, cutting him down to size.

By the time Theseus reached Athens, his reputation preceded him. But Athens faced a bigger problem than bandits.

The Minotaur and the Tribute

Years earlier, Aegeus's son from a previous marriage, Androgeus, had visited Crete and competed in King Minos's games. He won every event. Minos, suspicious of his success, sent Androgeus to kill a dangerous bull. Androgeus died.

Aegeus of Athens was blamed, though the details vary on why. Minos declared war. He had the more powerful navy, and Athens lost. As tribute, Athens had to send seven young men and seven young women to Crete every nine years (or every year, depending on the source). These fourteen were fed to the Minotaur.

The Minotaur was a monster. It was half-man, half-bull, the offspring of Minos's wife Pasiphaë and the sacred bull of Poseidon. Poseidon had given the bull to Minos to be sacrificed in the god's honor. But Minos, taken by its beauty, refused to sacrifice it. As punishment, Poseidon cursed Pasiphaë with an unnatural desire for the bull. With the help of the inventor Daedalus, she hid inside a wooden cow, allowing the bull to mate with her.

The Minotaur lived in the Labyrinth, a maze so complex that no one who entered ever found their way out. Daedalus had designed it specifically to trap the Minotaur.

When Theseus arrived in Athens, the time had come for another tribute. Theseus volunteered to be one of the fourteen, intending to kill the Minotaur and end the tribute forever.

Ariadne and the Thread

When Theseus arrived in Crete, Ariadne, the daughter of King Minos, saw him and fell in love. She knew what awaited him in the Labyrinth. No one had ever returned.

Desperate to save him, she went to Daedalus. He gave her a ball of thread and told her to tie it at the entrance, unwind it while moving in the maze, and follow it back to escape.

Ariadne gave the thread to Theseus. He entered the Labyrinth with the thirteen other Athenian youths. Inside, the air was still and strange. The stone passages twisted endlessly. He unwound the thread with each step, moving deeper and deeper into the darkness.

At the center, he met the Minotaur. They fought. Some say Theseus killed it with a sword. Others say he beat it to death with his fists or strangled it with a club. However it ended, the beast was slain.

Theseus slaying the Minotaur with Athena watching.[15]

Theseus followed the thread back and led the others out. All fourteen escaped.

Ariadne had betrayed her family and kingdom for Theseus. She had asked only one thing in return: take her to Athens and marry her. Theseus agreed. For the moment, the hero and the traitor sailed into freedom together.

The Betrayal of Ariadne

On the journey home from Crete, Theseus's ship stopped at the island of Naxos. What happened next varies wildly depending on the source.

In most versions, Theseus abandoned Ariadne while she slept on the shore. Why would he do this? Some say he fell out of love. Others claim that the gods intervened. Athena or Dionysus appeared in a dream or vision and commanded Theseus to leave her behind. Some versions offer no excuse at all.

Ariadne awoke alone. The sails of Theseus's ship had already vanished over the horizon. She had betrayed her father, fled her homeland, and saved his life—and he left her with nothing.

But then came Dionysus, god of wine and ecstasy. He found Ariadne weeping on the beach and was struck by her beauty and sorrow. He comforted her, loved her, and married her. To honor her, he placed her wedding crown among the stars as the constellation Corona Borealis.

Ariadne's story ends with immortality and love, but no version excuses Theseus's actions. Whether by negligence, pride, or obedience to the gods, he broke his promise.

The Black Sails

Before leaving Athens, Theseus promised his father that if he returned alive from Crete, he would change the black sails of his ship to white. Black sails meant death. White sails would signal victory.

But Theseus forgot. Or perhaps he was too distracted. Either way, as his ship approached Athens, the sails remained black.

Aegeus, waiting on a cliff above the sea, saw the black sails on the horizon. Believing his only son was dead, he was overcome with despair. He threw himself into the sea and drowned. Ever since, those waters have been known as the Aegean Sea.

Theseus returned home victorious, having slain the Minotaur and freed Athens from its tribute, but he entered the city as a king made by death, not by triumph. His father's death, caused by his own carelessness, marked the beginning of his reign and the end of his innocence.

The King of Athens

As king, Theseus unified the scattered villages of Attica into a single city-state, Athens. This wasn't just political propaganda. Archaeological evidence suggests some kind of political unification did happen in Athens's early history, though it probably did not happen in one dramatic moment.

According to Athenian tradition, Theseus established democratic reforms. He created the Panathenaic Festival, Athens's most important religious celebration. He divided citizens into classes based on wealth rather than birth. He supposedly coined the phrase "Nothing in excess," though this was also attributed to others.

Theseus went on other adventures as well. He joined Heracles on his expedition to the Amazons, the ninth labor. While Heracles fought for Hippolyta's belt, Theseus kidnapped the Amazon Antiope (or Hippolyta in some versions; the names get confusing). He brought her back to Athens and married her. She bore him a son, Hippolytus.

The Amazons weren't happy. They invaded Attica to get their queen back. The battle raged throughout Athens itself. Eventually, the Amazons were defeated, but Antiope died in the fighting, either killed by her own people or defending Athens with Theseus.

After Antiope's death, Theseus married Phaedra, the sister of Ariadne—yes, the woman he had abandoned. This went very badly.

Hippolytus, Theseus's son by Antiope, had grown into a handsome young man devoted to Artemis. He scorned Aphrodite and refused all romance. Aphrodite was insulted and took revenge by making Phaedra fall desperately in love with her stepson.

Phaedra tried to resist but eventually confessed her feelings to Hippolytus. He was horrified and rejected her. Phaedra, humiliated, hanged herself but left a note accusing Hippolytus of rape.

Theseus, believing the note, cursed his son. Poseidon, Theseus's divine father, honored the curse by sending a bull from the sea. It frightened Hippolytus's horses. His chariot crashed, and he was dragged to death.

Only after Hippolytus died did Theseus learn the truth. His wife had lied. His son had been innocent. Theseus had killed him based on a false accusation. This is one of the great tragedies that Euripides dramatized.

This wasn't the only mistake Theseus would make. His friendship with Pirithous, the king of the Lapiths of Larissa, led to his stupidest decision.

The two heroes had made a pact. They would each abduct a daughter of Zeus as a bride. First, they kidnapped Helen, who was still a child at the time. The plan was for Theseus to marry her when she came of age. He left her with his mother for safekeeping.

Pirithous decided he wanted to marry Persephone, queen of the underworld. The problem was that she was currently married to Hades. This idea was insane. But Theseus felt obligated to help.

They descended to the underworld and demanded Persephone. Hades, showing remarkable restraint, didn't kill them immediately. Instead, he invited them to sit and rest. When they sat down, they couldn't stand up. The chairs bound them.

They sat there for years, or forever, depending on the version. Heracles eventually descended to the underworld for his twelfth labor and freed Theseus, though Pirithous had to remain. Theseus returned to Athens weakened and humiliated.

Whatever happened to Helen? Well, her brothers, Castor and Pollux, eventually rescued her and drove Theseus from Athens. Theseus died in exile, thrown off a cliff by King Lycomedes of Scyros. The hero who had killed bandits, slain the Minotaur, and founded Athens died alone and forgotten.

Later, the Athenians "rediscovered" his bones and brought them back to Athens with great honors.

Jason and the Argonauts:
The First Great Road Trip in History

Jason's quest for the Golden Fleece might be the oldest "quest story" in Western literature. It is about a group of heroes that assembled for an impossible mission in a distant land. It's kind of like the *Ocean's Eleven* of ancient Greece.

The Usurped Throne

Jason's father, Aeson, was the rightful king of Iolcus. But Aeson's half-brother, Pelias, was the son of Poseidon and had ambitions beyond his birthright. He seized the throne, imprisoned Aeson, and tried to eliminate any rival heirs.

To protect her child, Aeson's wife faked Jason's death and secretly sent him away to be raised in safety. The infant was brought to Mount Pelion, where he was entrusted to the care of the centaur Chiron, the same teacher who trained Heracles, Achilles, and Asclepius.

When Jason came of age, he learned about his birthright. He decided to go to Iolcus to claim what was rightfully his.

On the way, he encountered an old woman stuck at a river, unable to cross. Jason carried her. The crossing was difficult, and he lost a sandal in the mud. The old woman was Hera in disguise. She was testing Jason's character. Impressed by his kindness, she became his patron.

Jason arrived in Iolcus wearing only one sandal. Pelias saw him and realized that he was there to fulfill the prophecy. But Pelias was clever. Instead of killing Jason outright, which would make him a tyrant, he sent Jason on an impossible quest.

"If you want the throne," he said, "prove you're worthy. Bring me the Golden Fleece."

The Golden Fleece came from a magical flying ram that had saved two children, Phrixus and Helle, from being sacrificed. Helle fell off during the flight and drowned. The sea was named the Hellespont after her. Phrixus reached Colchis and sacrificed the ram to Zeus. Its golden fleece was hung in a sacred grove, guarded by a dragon that never slept.

The fleece had magical properties. Whoever possessed it would have prosperity and power. Pelias wanted it but knew retrieving it was suicide. Sending Jason was a way to eliminate a rival while maintaining plausible deniability.

Assembling the Argonauts

Jason couldn't do this alone. He commissioned a ship, the *Argo*, and sent word throughout Greece that he was assembling a crew for the greatest adventure ever attempted.

The heroes who answered his call became known as the Argonauts. Here are some of the most famous:

- Heracles, the strongest man alive
- Orpheus, whose music could charm even stones
- Castor and Pollux, Helen's brothers and expert fighters
- Atalanta, the greatest female hunter (she only appears in some versions)
- Peleus, who would father Achilles
- Telamon, who would father Ajax
- Meleager, hero of the Calydonian Boar hunt
- Zetes and Calais, winged sons of the North Wind

Nearly every major hero of that generation joined. The *Argo* itself was special. It was built with timber from the sacred grove of Dodona, which gave the ship the ability to speak and prophesy.

The Journey

The voyage to Colchis was an adventure in itself. The Argonauts faced numerous obstacles.

The first stop was the island of Lemnos, which was populated only by women. The women had murdered all the men after they took Thracian concubines. The women welcomed the Argonauts, and the heroes stayed for months, fathering children. Only Heracles, never one for distractions, urged them to remember their quest and continue the journey.

At Cyzicus, they were welcomed by King Cyzicus. They left but were blown back by storms at night. In the darkness, the Cyzicans mistook them for pirates and attacked. The Argonauts fought back. By morning, they discovered they had accidentally killed Cyzicus and his men. They held elaborate funeral games in grief and guilt.

Soon after, they reached Mysia, where Heracles's young companion and lover, Hylas, left the group to fetch water from a spring. But Hylas never returned. The water nymphs who dwelled in the spring were entranced by his beauty and pulled him into the depths, either drowning him or transforming him to live with them forever. Heracles searched for days, calling out Hylas's name. He refused to leave without him. Eventually, the Argonauts had to move on. Heracles was left behind, abandoning the quest to continue his search.

The crew next encountered Phineus, a blind prophet cursed by the gods. Every time he tried to eat, Harpies (winged monsters) would swoop down and defile his food. The winged Argonauts, Zetes and Calais, gave chase and drove the Harpies away. In gratitude, Phineus offered them crucial advice on how to survive the next peril: the Symplegades, or the Clashing Rocks.

The Symplegades were two giant rocks that smashed together whenever a ship tried to pass between them, crushing vessels instantly. Following Phineus's advice, Jason released a dove. The rocks crashed together, clipping only the dove's tail feathers. As they pulled apart again, Jason gave the order to row with everything the men had. The *Argo* surged forward. The rocks closed just after the ship passed, shearing off only the stern ornament. From that day on, the Symplegades stood still. The path to Colchis was open.

Medea and the Tasks

When Jason reached Colchis, King Aeëtes had no intention of giving up the fleece. He set impossible conditions in the hopes that Jason would die trying to meet them. Jason must yoke two fire-breathing bronze bulls, plow a field, and sow it with dragon's teeth. From the teeth would spring an army of warriors that Jason would have to defeat. Only then would he get the fleece.

Jason accepted, although he had no idea how he would accomplish such a feat. Luckily for him, Aeëtes's daughter, Medea, saw Jason and fell in love. Hera and Aphrodite had arranged this.

Medea was a powerful sorceress, a priestess of Hecate. She gave Jason an ointment that would protect him from fire. She also told him how to defeat the warriors: throw a stone among them, and they would fight each other instead of him.

Jason yoked the bronze bulls, plowed the field, and sowed the dragon's teeth. When the warriors sprang up, he threw a rock among them. Confused, they attacked each other until all were dead.

Aeëtes had never intended to keep his word. Even after Jason survived the trials, the king delayed and schemed, planning to kill the Argonauts to prevent them from taking the fleece.

Knowing her father would betray them, Medea made a decision that could never be undone. She chose Jason over her family, her homeland, and the gods who protected Colchis.

Under the cover of night, Medea led Jason to the sacred grove of Ares, where the Golden Fleece hung from an ancient oak. The fleece was guarded by a colossal dragon that never slept, coiled around the tree.

Medea used her magic to drug the serpent into sleep. Some sources say she sang to it, while others say she poisoned it. However it happened, the guardian finally stilled.

Jason and Medea by John William Waterhouse.[16]

Jason took the fleece from the tree. He knew he had to move fast since Aeëtes would soon learn of what transpired. The men boarded the *Argo*, as did Medea and her younger brother, Absyrtus.

Aeëtes pursued them. To delay him, Medea did something horrific. She killed her brother, cut his body into pieces, and scattered them in the sea. Aeëtes had to stop and collect his son's body for proper burial, giving the Argonauts time to escape. This act showed the darkness that lurked in Medea.

The return journey was equally dangerous. They sailed into the western seas, where they encountered the Sirens, monstrous beings whose voices lured sailors to their deaths. Ships that strayed too close would crash onto jagged rocks as their crews, entranced by the song, leaped overboard.

But the Argonauts had Orpheus, the greatest mortal musician. As the Sirens began their deadly song, Orpheus drew his lyre and played a melody so beautiful and pure that it drowned out the Sirens' voices. The crew passed by safely.

Later, the *Argo* reached the deadly strait between Scylla and Charybdis—the same monstrous hazards Odysseus would face years later. On one side, Scylla, a many-headed beast, snatched sailors from their decks. On the other side was Charybdis, a monstrous whirlpool. It swallowed entire ships and spat them out wrecked and broken.

To navigate this deadly passage, the sea goddess Thetis, at Hera's request, guided the *Argo* by swimming alongside it to ensure the ship passed safely. The heroes rowed furiously, holding their course through crashing waves and roaring sea.

When they finally returned to Iolcus, Jason presented the Golden Fleece to Pelias. But Pelias refused to give up the throne.

Jason turned to Medea for comfort. She took revenge. She convinced Pelias's daughters that she could make their father young again. She demonstrated by cutting up an old ram and boiling it with herbs. The ram emerged as a young lamb. However, she had used magic. The daughters, convinced, cut up their father and boiled him. But he didn't come back. Pelias's son drove Jason and Medea out of Iolcus.

The Tragedy of Jason and Medea

After being exiled from Iolcus, Jason and Medea fled to Corinth, where they were received as honored guests. For years, they lived in peace. They had children, and for a time, it seemed their bloody past had been left behind.

But Jason's ambitions had not died. Eventually, he sought to marry Glauce (also called Creusa), the daughter of King Creon of Corinth. It was a calculated move. By marrying into the royal family, Jason hoped to secure power, position, and a legitimate future for himself, even if it meant discarding Medea, who had sacrificed everything for him.

Jason justified his betrayal as a political necessity. He claimed the new marriage would benefit their children. Medea saw it for what it was: a profound humiliation, a betrayal not only of love but of everything she had done for him.

She plotted her revenge carefully.

Pretending to accept the situation, Medea sent Glauce a wedding gift: a robe woven with gold and a delicate crown. Glauce accepted it eagerly.

But the gifts were cursed. The moment Glauce put on the robe, flames erupted from the fabric, fusing to her skin and burning her alive. When her father, King Creon, tried to save her, the flames consumed him as well.

Still, Medea was not finished.

She knew that nothing would wound Jason more deeply than the loss of his children. And so, she killed them with her own hands. When Jason stormed into their home to stop her, it was too late. The bodies were gone.

Medea escaped in a chariot drawn by dragons, sent by her grandfather Helios, god of the sun. She took the children's bodies with her so that Jason would be unable to bury them.

Jason was left with nothing. He grew old alone and bitter. According to legend, he died when a piece of the *Argo*'s rotting hull fell on him as he sat beneath it, remembering his glory days.

The quest for the Golden Fleece was successful. But Jason's life was a tragedy, destroyed by his own betrayal of the woman who had sacrificed everything for him.

These heroes—Heracles, Perseus, Theseus, and Jason—were the greatest of their age. They killed monsters, completed legendary quests, and achieved glory that echoes through the millennia.

Yet power wasn't enough. Divine help was often necessary. And even with supernatural

Jason and the Golden Fleece *by Bertel Thorvaldsen.*[17]

assistance, they suffered terrible costs. They hurt the people who loved them. Many died badly.

Heroes achieved great things, but heroism didn't necessarily bring happiness. Glory didn't mean peace. A person couldn't outrun fate, escape their own flaws, or avoid the consequences of their choices.

The gods gave heroes power. But they didn't give them wisdom.

Chapter 5: Love, Hubris, and "Oops" Moments

The hero stories are about strength, courage, and endurance. They're epic and grand. But Greek mythology also told more personal stories, tales about what happens when mortals and gods make very human mistakes.

These are stories about love and its complications, about pride and its consequences, about wishes that backfire and beauty that destroys.

The Greeks had a word for excessive pride that violated social order: hubris. In ancient Greece, hubris wasn't just arrogance. It was a legal term that meant intentionally shaming someone of a lower status to assert your dominance or violating the boundaries that kept society functioning. The gods punished hubris, but so did Athenian courts.

Cupid (Eros) and Psyche: A Story of Trust and Soul

This is one of the few Greek myths with a happy ending. It's a love story, but it's not a simple one. It's about trust, betrayal, impossible tasks, and whether love can survive when you can't see the person you're loving.

Psyche was a princess, the youngest of three daughters. She was so beautiful that people stopped worshiping Aphrodite and instead brought offerings to her, calling her the new goddess of beauty.

This was a massive mistake. You don't steal worship from Aphrodite.

Aphrodite was furious. She called her son Eros, Cupid, and ordered him to make Psyche fall in love with the ugliest, most despicable creature on earth. Eros took his bow and his arrows. His golden arrows caused love, and his lead arrows caused revulsion.

He found Psyche sleeping. He prepared to shoot her with a golden arrow aimed at some horrible monster. But as he looked at her, he accidentally pricked himself with his own arrow. And he fell in love with Psyche instantly.

Eros couldn't tell his mother what happened. Instead, he decided to claim Psyche for himself.

Psyche's beauty became a curse. No man would marry her. They worshiped her from afar but were too intimidated to court her. Her sisters were less beautiful, but both married kings. Psyche remained alone.

Her father, desperate, consulted the Oracle at Delphi. The Oracle's answer was terrifying. Dress Psyche in funeral clothes and take her to a rocky mountaintop. There, a monster will claim her as his bride. This "husband" was so terrible that even the gods feared him.

The family, grief-stricken, did as commanded. They dressed Psyche in wedding clothes that looked like funeral garments and led her to a desolate crag. They left her there alone, weeping as they departed.

But the Oracle had been manipulated by Eros. The "monster" was him.

Psyche and Love by William-Adolphe Bouguereau.[18]

As Psyche stood alone on the mountain, the West Wind, Zephyrus, gently lifted her and carried her down to a beautiful valley. There stood a magnificent palace, seemingly empty but filled with invisible servants who attended to her every need.

That night, in complete darkness, Psyche's mysterious husband came to her. He spoke kindly. His voice was gentle and reassuring. He was loving and tender. But he made one demand: she must never try to see his face. If she ever looked at him, if she ever brought light into their chamber, he would have to leave forever. Their marriage would be over.

Psyche agreed. What choice did she have? Night after night, her husband visited in the darkness. They talked for hours. He told her about the world, about philosophy, about beauty. She grew to love him deeply, not for his appearance, which she'd never seen, but for his mind, his kindness, and his soul.

Days passed in luxury. The invisible servants gave her everything she wanted. Musicians played without being seen. Delicious food appeared on the tables. Baths were drawn. Clothes were laid out. The palace was paradise.

But she was lonely. Psyche had everything except real company. She missed her family desperately. She worried they thought she was dead.

She begged her husband to let her family visit. He was reluctant. He warned her, "Your sisters will bring trouble. They'll plant doubts in your mind. They'll make you question what we have. Please, don't let them visit."

But Psyche pleaded. She promised she wouldn't listen to anything negative they said. She just wanted to see them once, to let them know she was alive and happy.

Her husband finally agreed, but his warnings continued. "Be careful. They will try to poison your happiness. Don't trust their advice."

Psyche's sisters came, carried by the West Wind just as Psyche had been. When they saw the magnificent palace, which was far grander than their own royal homes, they were consumed by jealousy.

Psyche greeted them with joy, showing them the palace, the gardens, and the treasures. She told them about her wonderful husband who visited her each night, of how he loved her and treated her kindly.

"But you've never seen him?" her eldest sister asked, her voice dripping with false concern.

"No," Psyche admitted. "He comes only in darkness. But he's wonderful. His voice is beautiful. He's gentle and loving."

The sisters exchanged meaningful glances. "Psyche," the second sister said, taking her hand. "We love you. We're worried about you. Don't you remember what the Oracle said? You were supposed to marry a monster so terrible that even the gods fear him."

"But he's not a monster," Psyche protested. "He's kind. He takes care of me."

"That's what he wants you to think," the first sister insisted. "Why else would he hide his face? If he were truly handsome and kind, wouldn't he want you to see him? Wouldn't he be proud to show himself?"

The doubts started small. What if he's deformed? What if he's hideous? What if he's testing you?

Then the fears escalated. "We've heard stories," one sister whispered. "About serpents that can take human form. They speak in beautiful voices. They charm their victims. They fatten them up, make them comfortable. And then..."

"Then what?" Psyche asked, her heart racing.

"They devour them. Psyche, you might be living with a giant serpent. It's waiting until you're pregnant. Then it will eat both you and the child."

Psyche tried to defend her husband. She insisted he couldn't be a monster. But the sisters were relentless. They wept. They begged. They painted terrifying pictures. "We couldn't live with ourselves if something happened to you and we hadn't warned you."

Finally, they gave her a plan. "Tonight, after he falls asleep, light a lamp. Just look at him once. If he's truly what you think he is, you'll know we were wrong, and you can blow out the lamp. But if he's a monster, you'll need this." They gave her a sharp knife. "Cut off his head while he sleeps. Save yourself."

After they left, Psyche sat alone, her mind churning. She didn't want to believe them. But the doubt had taken root. What if they were right? What if she were in danger? Wouldn't a loving husband want to be seen? Why all the secrecy?

That night, when her husband fell asleep beside her, Psyche made her decision. She had to know. She lit an oil lamp and held it over the bed.

And she saw the most beautiful being she'd ever encountered. Eros lay sleeping, his golden wings folded, his face perfect beyond description. She saw his bow and arrows beside the bed. This was no monster. This was a god.

Psyche stood there, stunned by his beauty, flooded with love and relief. But as she leaned closer, a drop of hot oil from the lamp fell on Eros's shoulder.

He woke instantly. He saw the lamp in her hand. Without a word, he rose and flew away.

As he left, he said, "Love cannot live where there is no trust." Then he vanished.

The palace disappeared. The invisible servants were gone. Psyche was alone on a barren hillside, having lost everything because she doubted.

Psyche was devastated. She had betrayed the one who loved her. She decided she had to win him back or die trying.

She prayed to Aphrodite, asking for a chance to make amends. Aphrodite, still furious that her son had married the mortal who'd stolen her worship, agreed, but only if Psyche completed a series of impossible tasks.

First, Aphrodite poured out a massive pile of mixed seeds: wheat, barley, millet, poppy, chickpeas, lentils, and beans. Psyche had to sort them by nightfall.

It was an impossible task. But ants took pity on Psyche and sorted every seed perfectly before sunset.

Next, Psyche had to retrieve the golden fleece from vicious divine sheep. A river reed whispered advice to her. "Wait until the afternoon when the sheep cross the river, then collect the fleece snagged on bushes." Psyche did this and succeeded.

Aphrodite, shocked that Psyche had made it this far, demanded that she fill a crystal flask with water from the River Styx, which flowed from an inaccessible cliff guarded by dragons. Zeus's eagle took the flask, flew to the spring, and brought it back.

Psyche's last task was to descend to the underworld and retrieve a box of beauty ointment from Persephone. She was not to open it.

A talking tower told Psyche how to navigate Hades safely. She must bring two coins for Charon and two honey cakes for Cerberus. She should not help anyone, and she definitely should not open the box.

Psyche followed the instructions perfectly. She descended, got the box, and returned to the surface.

But then, as she was holding the box, she thought, "I must look terrible. If I use just a little, I'll be beautiful when I see Eros."

She opened the box. It contained the Sleep of Death. Psyche collapsed, apparently lifeless.

Eros, who had been recovering from his burn and his broken heart, discovered what had happened. He'd never stopped loving Psyche. He flew to her, wiped the Sleep of Death from her face and put it back in the box, and revived her with a prick from one of his arrows.

Then he flew to Olympus and begged Zeus for help. Zeus, charmed by the love story and annoyed at Aphrodite's cruelty, agreed. He made Psyche immortal and formally married her to Eros.

Aphrodite had to accept it. Psyche became a goddess. She and Eros had a daughter named Voluptas (Pleasure in Latin, Hedone in Greek). Hedone became the personification of pleasure and joy, not moral failing or excess, but the feeling of delight itself. The word "hedonism" comes from her name, though the philosophical concept developed much later.

The story ends with a wedding feast on Olympus. Love and the Soul, Eros and Psyche (their names literally mean "love" and "soul") were finally united.

Icarus and Phaethon:
The Dangers of Flying Too High (Literally)

Greek mythology is full of people who reach too high and fall. Two stories stand out the most: Icarus, who literally flew too close to the sun, and Phaethon, who drove the sun chariot itself. Both died because they couldn't accept their limitations.

Icarus: The Boy Who Flew

Icarus's father was Daedalus, the greatest inventor and craftsman in all of Greece. Daedalus could build anything. He'd studied under Athena herself. He created sculptures so lifelike that people swore they could move. Later writers even credited him with inventing the tools of his trade—the saw, the ax, and the level—though these attributions come from much later sources like Diodorus Siculus. Daedalus's mind was brilliant, his hands were skilled, and his creations were legendary.

But Daedalus had a dark past. In Athens, his nephew and apprentice Talos had shown signs of genius that might surpass even him. Consumed by jealousy, Daedalus pushed Talos off the Acropolis. Athena, pitying the boy, transformed him into a bird mid-fall. Talos became the partridge, which flies close to the ground and never soars high, supposedly out of fear of that original fall. Daedalus was caught and exiled from Athens.

He fled to Crete, where King Minos welcomed him and put his skills to use. Daedalus built many wonders for Minos, including a hollow wooden cow that allowed Queen Pasiphaë to mate with Poseidon's bull, resulting in the Minotaur. He built the Labyrinth to contain the Minotaur, a maze so complex that even Daedalus himself could barely navigate it.

After Theseus killed the Minotaur and escaped using the thread Daedalus had suggested to Ariadne, Minos was furious. He knew Daedalus had helped. As punishment, Minos imprisoned Daedalus and his young son Icarus in the very Labyrinth Daedalus had built.

But Daedalus had designed the Labyrinth. Escaping the maze was the easy part. The problem was escaping Crete. Minos controlled the island completely. Every ship was searched. Guards watched every port. Minos had declared that Daedalus would never leave Crete alive.

Daedalus studied the problem. Any escape route by land was blocked. The sea was blocked. That left only one option.

Daedalus realized that Minos controlled the land and sea, but not the sky.

He watched the birds flying freely over the Mediterranean. He studied how they flew, how their wings caught the air, and how they soared and glided. He collected feathers from the birds that nested in the Labyrinth, large feathers from eagles and gulls, small ones from sparrows and doves. He arranged them from smallest to largest, overlapping them like natural wings. Daedalus bound them together with thread and sealed them with wax from the honeycombs the bees made in the Labyrinth's upper chambers.

He created two pairs of wings, measuring them carefully against Icarus's shoulders and his own. He taught Icarus how to move his arms to catch the air, how to angle the wings to rise or fall, and how to read the wind. They practiced in the Labyrinth's courtyards, making short hops and learning how to balance.

Before they fled, Daedalus gave Icarus explicit instructions. "Listen to me carefully. Fly at medium height. This is crucial. If you fly too low, the sea spray will soak the feathers, and the wings will become too heavy. You'll fall into the water and drown. If you fly too high, the sun's heat will melt the wax holding the feathers. The wings will fall apart, and you'll plummet to your death. Stay between the sea and the sun. Follow me. Follow my path exactly. Don't get distracted. Don't get clever. Just follow me. Do you understand?"

Icarus promised he understood.

They strapped on the wings. Daedalus went first, launching himself from the Labyrinth's highest tower. The wings caught the air, and he soared. It worked.

Icarus followed. His wings held. He was flying! For the first time in human history, a person was flying through the air like a bird.

They flew over Crete. People below looked up in astonishment, pointing and shouting. Some thought they were seeing gods.

At first, Icarus obeyed his father carefully. He flew at the right height, following Daedalus's path. But the thrill of flight was intoxicating. He was flying, like a bird, like a god. The world spread out below him, tiny ships on a glittering sea, islands like scattered gems, mountains and valleys stretching to the horizon.

He flew a little higher. The air was thinner, colder, and clearer. He could see farther. He went higher still. The wind felt different up here, rushing past him, wild and free. He felt limitless, untouchable, free from every constraint that had ever bound him.

He flew higher. And higher. The sun grew larger and became hotter, more brilliant. It felt like he was approaching divinity itself.

The wax began to soften. Small drops started falling like tears.

Daedalus, flying ahead on the planned route, looked back and saw Icarus climbing higher and higher, a tiny silhouette against the sun. He shouted warnings, screaming his son's name, but Icarus couldn't hear or didn't listen. He was too far away, too caught up in the glory of flight.

The wax melted. Feathers began peeling away, floating down like snow. Icarus felt the wings loosening. He looked at his arms and saw gaps appearing in the feathers. Panic struck him like lightning.

He flapped desperately, trying to stay aloft, but there was nothing left to hold the air. The wings disintegrated completely. Icarus hung in the air for one impossible moment, his arms still spread, still hoping.

Then he fell.

He plummeted toward the sea, his scream cut short as he hit the water and sank beneath the waves.

Daedalus circled back, calling his son's name, searching the water. He found only floating feathers. The Greeks named that part of the Aegean the Icarian Sea, turning a tragedy into a permanent memorial.

The Lament for Icarus by Herbert James Draper.[19]

Daedalus reached Sicily, carrying unbearable grief. He built a temple to Apollo and hung up his wings as an offering, swearing never to fly again.

"Don't fly too close to the sun" became shorthand for "don't overreach." Icarus died because he was young, excited, and forgot that the rules applied to him. His father gave him perfect instructions. Icarus just didn't follow them.

Phaethon: The Boy Who Drove the Sun

Phaethon was the son of the sun god Helios and the Oceanid nymph Clymene. He grew up in the mortal world with his mother, not knowing his divine father. When he was old enough to understand, Clymene told him the truth: his father was Helios himself, who drove the sun across the sky each day.

Phaethon was proud of his heritage. He told everyone about it. But the other children didn't believe him. They mocked him relentlessly. "Your father is the sun? Sure he is. And my father is Zeus!" They laughed at him, called him a liar, and said his mother had made up the story to hide the fact that he was fatherless.

Phaethon, furious and hurt, went to his mother in tears. "They don't believe me. They say I'm making it up. Is it true? Is Helios really my father?"

Clymene swore it was true. She raised her hands to the sky and called on Helios as witness. "I swear by your father himself. If I'm lying, may I never see the sun again. If you still don't believe me, go to him. Travel east to the palace where the sun rises. Ask Helios yourself. He'll tell you the truth."

Phaethon decided to make the journey. He traveled east for days, following the sun's path, until he reached the edge of the world where night gives way to dawn.

There, he found Helios's palace, a structure so magnificent it made mortal palaces look like ruins. The walls were silver and gold. The doors were bronze and glowed like fire. The roof was ivory and gems. Everything gleamed with light so bright it hurt to look at it directly.

Inside, the palace was even more stunning. Helios sat on a throne made of blazing emeralds, surrounded by the Hours, the goddesses who marked each hour of the day, and the Days, the Months, the Years, and the Seasons. Spring was crowned with flowers. Summer wore ripening grain. Autumn dripped with grape juice. Winter's hair was white with frost.

Phaethon, overwhelmed, shielded his eyes. Helios saw the boy and immediately knew him. The divine blood was obvious. He removed the crown of burning rays from his head so Phaethon could approach safely.

"Come closer," Helios said gently. "You are my son. I know you. What do you need?"

Phaethon, his voice shaking, asked, "Are you really my father? The other boys don't believe me. They mock me and call me a liar. Will you acknowledge me publicly?"

Helios smiled sadly. "Yes. You are my son. And to prove it, I swear by the River Styx that I'll grant you any request you make. Ask for anything, and I'll give it to you."

This was a serious oath. The River Styx was the most powerful force in the universe. Even gods couldn't break oaths sworn by the Styx.

Phaethon made his request. "Let me drive your chariot for one day. Let me pull the sun across the sky so everyone will see that I'm truly your son."

The smile vanished from Helios's face. He immediately regretted his rash oath. He begged Phaethon to ask for anything else. "Ask for wealth beyond measure. Ask for a kingdom. Ask for immortality. Ask for wisdom, for power, for anything else. Just not this."

He tried to explain the danger. "The horses are wild, born from fire and fury. They barely obey me, and I'm a god who has driven them for eons. The path is treacherous. At dawn, the ascent is so steep that even the horses struggle. At noon, you're at the highest point of heaven. I look down and fear, and I've done this every day since time began. In the evening, the descent is sharp and requires perfect control to avoid crashing into the western ocean. And you're mortal. You don't have my strength."

Phaethon wouldn't listen. "You swore by the Styx. You have to let me try."

Helios tried another approach. "Even Zeus doesn't drive my chariot, and he's the king of the gods. If the mightiest Olympian won't attempt it, how can you, a mortal boy?"

But Phaethon was determined. He saw this as his chance to prove himself, to show everyone that he truly was the son of the sun. "You swore. You can't break this oath."

Helios, trapped by his own promise, had no choice. With a heavy heart, he prepared the chariot. The four horses, Pyrois, Eos, Aethon, and Phlegon, were barely restrained by the grooms. They breathed fire. Their eyes blazed. Their hooves struck sparks from the golden floor.

Dawn opened the doors of the palace. The stars fled. The night withdrew. Helios rubbed sacred oil on Phaethon's face to protect him from the heat and placed the crown of rays on his head.

He gave some final instructions. "Hold the reins firmly but gently. The horses will try to bolt. They always do at first. Don't use the whip at all. Their natural energy is the problem, not a lack of speed. Keep to the established path. You'll see the wheel ruts in the sky. Stay in them. Don't climb too high or sink too low. Don't look at the constellations or get distracted. And whatever you do, don't panic. If you panic, you're finished."

Phaethon climbed into the chariot. The reins felt strange in his hands. The horses sensed an unfamiliar driver immediately. They stamped and snorted, eager to run.

The doors opened wide, and the horses bolted.

Phaethon pulled the reins, but the horses didn't respond. They veered off the established path immediately, climbing too steeply, too fast. The chariot lurched and swayed.

The horses sensed they carried a lightweight, weak driver. They knew they could do whatever they wanted. They bolted in different directions, pulling the chariot erratically across the sky.

First, they climbed far too high. The constellations Phaethon had heard about all his life were suddenly all around him. The Great Bear tried to attack the chariot. The Scorpion raised its stinger, dripping poison. Phaethon screamed and jerked the reins, and the horses plunged downward.

The earth below grew cold as the sun pulled away. Frost formed. Rivers began to freeze. People huddled in their homes, shivering, wondering why the sun had abandoned them.

Then the horses dove too low. Mountains burst into flame. Forests ignited in an instant. Rivers boiled, then dried up completely, their beds cracking and splitting. Cities caught fire. People ran screaming, but there was nowhere to hide from the sun when it came that close.

The Greeks used this myth to explain features of their world. The Sahara Desert hadn't always been barren sand. Libya had been green and lush before Phaethon's disastrous ride. The sun scorched it permanently, turning fertile land into an endless desert. The Greeks claimed that the people of Ethiopia had their skin darkened by the flames that day. These were etiological myths, stories invented to explain natural phenomena and human diversity through the Greeks' own limited cultural lens. By modern standards, these explanations are problematic, but they reveal how the ancient Greeks attempted to make sense of the world they encountered through trade and travel.

Great rivers boiled away to almost nothing. The ocean itself began to steam. Poseidon rose from the deep and shouted at the sky, but even he couldn't stop the destruction.

Mountain nymphs watched their homes burn. Forest spirits fled as ancient groves were reduced to ash. Animals of all kinds ran in terror from the heat.

Gaia, the Earth herself, couldn't take any more. She lifted her head, mountains heaving upward, and cried out to Zeus. Her voice was parched, choked with smoke. "If this continues, everything will burn. The sea will boil away. The sky will catch fire. We'll return to Chaos. You must stop this!"

Zeus looked down from Olympus and saw the world burning. He saw Phaethon in the chariot, overwhelmed and terrified, unable to control the horses. The boy was going to destroy everything, not out of malice but out of simple inability.

Zeus had no choice. He had to act. He couldn't reason with the boy. Phaethon was beyond hearing. He couldn't stop the horses. They were in a complete frenzy. There was only one option.

Zeus raised his arm. Thunder rolled across the sky. He hurled a thunderbolt.

The bolt struck Phaethon square in the chest, killing him instantly. The boy's hair burst into flames. His body tumbled from the chariot, falling through the sky like a shooting star, his arms and legs spread wide, trailing smoke and fire.

He crashed into the River Eridanus, possibly the Po River in northern Italy, his body still burning as it hit the water. The river hissed and steamed. Phaethon sank beneath the surface.

The horses, now free of any driver, knew their route by instinct. They returned to the established path and rushed to complete their journey, bringing what remained of the day to its proper conclusion before returning to Helios's palace, exhausted.

Helios, seeing what had happened, was devastated. His son was dead. The world was scarred. It was all his fault for making that oath.

He refused to drive his chariot the next day. The world remained in darkness. Zeus and the other gods came to him, begging him to resume his duty. "If you don't drive the sun, everything will freeze and die."

Helios wept. His tears fell to the earth and became amber, golden drops of divine sorrow that washed up on riverbanks. But he knew his duty. The sun had to rise. He returned to his chariot.

Meanwhile, Phaethon's body had been found by the nymphs of the Eridanus. They buried him on the riverbank with full honors, marking his grave with an epitaph: "Here lies Phaethon, driver of his father's chariot. He could not control it, but he dared greatly."

His sisters, the Heliades, mourned him intensely, weeping by his grave day and night. The gods took pity and transformed them into poplar trees that would stand forever by the river. Their tears continued to fall as sap, which hardened into amber. To this day, amber is found along certain rivers. They are supposedly the solidified tears of Phaethon's sisters, who are still grieving.

His close friend Cygnus had also mourned him, diving into the river again and again, searching for Phaethon's body, refusing to accept his death. The gods transformed Cygnus into a swan, a bird that dives in rivers and seems forever to search beneath the water.

Helios loved his son and would have given him anything. However, Phaethon demanded the one thing that would kill him, and a divine oath forced Helios to allow it.

King Midas and Narcissus:

Be Careful What You Wish For and Who You Look At

Greek myths loved to punish people for being greedy and selfish. Two stories stand out for their warnings about desire.

King Midas: The Golden Touch

Midas was a king of Phrygia, in modern-day Turkey. He was wealthy, powerful, and generally a decent person. But he had one major flaw: he loved gold more than anything.

The story begins when Midas helped the satyr Silenus, who was Dionysus's companion and tutor. Silenus had gotten drunk, as usual, and wandered away from Dionysus's entourage. He ended up in Midas's rose garden, where Midas's servants found him passed out.

Midas recognized Silenus and treated him as an honored guest for ten days, hosting feasts and entertainment. When he returned Silenus to Dionysus, the god was so grateful that he offered Midas any reward he wanted.

Midas, thinking of his love for gold, made his wish. "Let everything I touch turn to gold."

Dionysus tried to dissuade him. This was clearly a terrible idea. But Midas insisted. And Dionysus, bound by his promise, granted the wish.

At first, Midas was ecstatic. He touched a stone, and it became gold. He touched a branch, and it turned to gold. He touched a pillar of his palace, making it solid gold. He was going to be the richest man in the world.

Then he tried to eat.

The bread turned to gold in his hands. The wine turned to gold as it touched his lips. He couldn't eat. He couldn't drink. Everything he touched became hard, cold, inedible metal.

He called for his daughter. She ran to embrace him. The moment he touched her, she transformed into a golden statue.

Midas, horrified and starving, realized he'd made a terrible mistake. He prayed to Dionysus, begging for mercy.

Dionysus took pity on him. He told Midas to wash in the River Pactolus. Midas did, and the golden touch washed away into the river. His daughter was restored. He could eat and drink again.

The river's sands turned to gold from Midas's touch, which is why the Pactolus was famous for gold deposits in ancient times.

Midas learned his lesson about gold. But he didn't learn about humility.

Later, Midas judged a musical contest between Apollo and Pan. Apollo played his refined lyre. Pan played his simple reed pipes. Midas declared Pan the winner, saying he preferred the rustic, honest music to Apollo's sophisticated performance.

Apollo was furious. As punishment, he gave Midas donkey ears.

Midas hid the ears under a Phrygian cap and swore his barber to secrecy. But the barber couldn't keep quiet about such a juicy secret. He dug a hole in the ground and whispered into it. "King Midas has donkey ears!" Relieved, he filled in the hole.

But reeds grew from that spot. Whenever the wind blew, the reeds whispered, "King Midas has donkey ears ... King Midas has donkey ears..."

The secret spread throughout the kingdom. Midas lived in humiliation for the rest of his life.

The moral is to be careful what you wish for. What seems like the perfect gift can become a curse. More isn't always better. And definitely don't insult Apollo's music.

Narcissus: The Boy Who Loved Himself

Narcissus was the most beautiful young man anyone had ever seen. His parents, the river god Cepheus and the nymph Liriope, consulted the blind prophet Tiresias shortly after his birth. They asked, "Will our son live a long life?"

Tiresias gave a strange answer. "Yes, if he never knows himself."

They didn't understand the prophecy. How could anyone not know themselves? But Tiresias was never wrong, so they accepted it.

Narcissus grew up extraordinarily beautiful. As a teenager, both men and women fell in love with him. He couldn't walk through the forest without someone confessing their feelings. But Narcissus rejected everyone. He wasn't cruel at first; he was just completely uninterested in love or romance. He seemed to care for nothing and no one except hunting.

Among those who loved him was the nymph Echo. But Echo had a problem that made courtship impossible.

Echo's story begins with Hera's jealousy. Zeus, as usual, was having an affair, this time with mountain nymphs. Whenever Hera came searching for him, Echo would waylay her with long, entertaining conversations, giving Zeus time to hide his lovers and cover his tracks.

Hera eventually realized what Echo was doing. Furious, she cursed her. "You love to talk? Fine. But you'll never speak your own words again. You can only repeat the end of what others say. Let's see you distract me with that."

The curse took effect immediately. Echo could no longer start a conversation or speak her own thoughts. She could only echo the final words or phrases others spoke, a poetic punishment that left her able to communicate but never to express herself.

When Echo saw Narcissus hunting in the forest, she fell desperately in love. She tried to approach him, but she couldn't speak first. She had to wait for him to say something.

Narcissus, sensing he wasn't alone, called out, "Is anyone there?"

Echo, overjoyed to finally engage, repeated, "Anyone there ... there ... there..."

Narcissus looked around, confused. "Come to me!"

Echo, thrilled, repeated, "Come to me!" and rushed toward him from the trees, her arms outstretched.

When Narcissus saw her emerging from the shadows, he recoiled. He didn't know her. He hadn't asked for this. "Don't touch me! I'd rather die than let you have me!" He turned and ran.

Echo tried to follow, tried to explain, but all she could do was repeat his own words: "Let you have me ... have me ... have me..." The words mocked her, turning her genuine feelings into hollow repetition.

Heartbroken and humiliated, Echo fled deep into the mountains. She stopped eating. She stopped sleeping. She wasted away from grief and shame. Her flesh disappeared, and her bones turned to stone. Only her voice remained, a voice that could merely repeat others' words, hiding in caves and valleys, forever unable to express her own feelings.

But Echo wasn't Narcissus's only rejected lover. A young man who had also been spurned prayed to Nemesis, goddess of revenge and retribution. "May he who loves not others love himself alone."

Nemesis heard the prayer. She decided Narcissus needed to learn what it felt like to love someone who could never love him back.

One day, after a hunt, Narcissus came upon a perfectly still pool of water in a secluded grove. The pool was fed by a spring and surrounded by rocks and trees that protected it from the wind. Its surface was like polished glass.

Narcissus, hot and thirsty, knelt to drink. He saw a face in the water, the most beautiful face he'd ever seen. Perfect features, perfect skin, eyes like jewels. He fell in love instantly.

He reached out. The water rippled, and the face disappeared. He tried to kiss it. The image shattered. He spoke to it. It seemed to answer, lips moving in sync with his, but made no sound.

Slowly, terribly, Narcissus realized he was looking at himself. His own reflection. He was in love with his own image, and he could never possess it. Every attempt to touch it made it disappear.

Knowledge should have freed him. But it didn't. He couldn't look away. Logic meant nothing against the force of that love.

"Why do you elude me?" he asked his reflection. "I'm here. You're here. When I smile, you smile. When I reach out, you reach out. We're perfect for each other. Why can't we be together?"

Narcissus stayed by the pool, refusing to eat or drink or sleep. He wasted away, consumed by love for someone who couldn't love him back. His beauty faded. His body became thin. But still he stared.

As he was dying, he looked one last time at his reflection and whispered, "Goodbye, beloved." Echo whispered back, "Goodbye, beloved."

Narcissus died beside the pool. When the nymphs came to collect his body for burial, they found no corpse. Instead, where he had lain, a flower grew, a white narcissus with a golden center, bending over the water as if admiring its own reflection.

The flower still grows near water, forever looking down, forever in love with its own image.

Tiresias's prophecy had been fulfilled. Narcissus lived only as long as he didn't know himself. Once he saw his own face, once he truly knew himself, he was doomed.

The story is brutal. Narcissus's punishment fits his crime perfectly. He rejected everyone's love, so he was cursed to love someone who would reject him.

The myth gave us the word "narcissism," excessive self-love and self-absorption. But the original Narcissus didn't start out vain. He just didn't care about anyone. His curse made him care but only about himself, forever.

The Warnings

The Greeks understood that getting exactly what you want is often the worst thing that can happen. What seems desirable from a distance becomes unbearable up close.

The lesson was to think carefully about what you want. Be careful whom you reject, whom you insult, and what you take for granted.

Because the gods are watching. And they have a terrible sense of humor.

Chapter 6: The Dark Side—The Underworld

Death was inevitable in Greek mythology. Heroes could accomplish impossible tasks, but they all died eventually. Gods were immortal, but everyone else had an appointment with Hades.

The Greeks didn't sugarcoat death. They didn't promise paradise for good behavior or torment for sin. The afterlife was mostly just there. It was a shadowy existence underground. You went there when you died, regardless of how you lived. For most people, death meant becoming a shade, a pale, insubstantial copy of your former self, wandering forever in dim twilight.

But the underworld wasn't simple. It had rulers, rivers, regions, and rules. Understanding Greek views on death means understanding where the dead went and what happened to them there.

Geography of the Dead: Styx, Tartarus, and the Elysian Fields

The underworld, often called Hades after its ruler, though the Greeks had many names for it, was a vast realm beneath the earth. Getting there required crossing boundaries that separated the living from the dead.

The Rivers of the Underworld

Five rivers flowed through the underworld, each with its own properties and meaning.

The River Styx was the most famous. Its name meant "hatred" or "dread." The Styx formed the boundary between the world of the living and the world of the dead, wrapping around the underworld multiple times.

The Styx had immense power over the gods. Oaths sworn by the River Styx couldn't be broken, even by Zeus. When a god swore by the Styx, they were binding themselves to the most ancient and powerful force in the cosmos. Breaking such an oath brought terrible consequences. The god would lose their voice and breath, fall into a coma-like state for a year, and then be exiled from Olympus for nine more years.

The River Acheron was the "river of woe" or "river of sorrow." While many people today think of Charon ferrying souls across the Styx, many ancient Greek sources actually place him on the Acheron. The ferryman operated his crossing here, charging one coin, an obol, for passage. This is why Greeks placed coins on the eyes or in the mouth of the dead during burial. Without payment, Charon refused to ferry you across.

Charon didn't take just anyone. You had to be properly buried. If your body were left unburied, your soul couldn't cross. This made proper burial sacred to the Greeks. Even enemies deserved burial. Leaving a body to rot was a profound violation that trapped the soul in limbo. The consequences of being unburied varied by source and time period. Later Roman writers like Virgil specified a hundred-year wait, but earlier Greek sources simply emphasized the catastrophic offense to the gods and the soul's eternal restlessness.

The River Cocytus was the "river of lamentation." It was formed from the tears of those who died unjustly or unburied. The name comes from the wailing sounds that rose from its waters.

The River Phlegethon was the "river of fire." It flowed with flames instead of water, surrounding Tartarus and keeping the worst criminals contained. The heat was so intense that even approaching it was dangerous.

The River Lethe was the "river of forgetfulness" or "river of oblivion." Souls who drank from it forgot their mortal lives completely. Some sources say all souls drank from Lethe before being reincarnated. Others say only certain souls drank, those who needed to forget their suffering before moving on.

The Gates and the Guardian

After crossing the Styx, souls encountered the gates of Hades. These gates were guarded by Cerberus, the three-headed dog.

Cerberus was massive. Some sources even say he had fifty or a hundred heads, a serpent for a tail, and snakes growing from his back. He was friendly to incoming souls. His job was to let the dead in, not keep them out. But he prevented anyone from leaving. The dead stayed dead.

A few heroes managed to get past Cerberus. Heracles wrestled him into submission as his twelfth labor. Orpheus charmed him with music. The Sibyl (prophetesses or oracles) who guided Aeneas drugged him with honey cakes. But these were exceptional cases. For normal souls, Cerberus was a one-way gate.

The Regions of the Underworld

Once past Cerberus, souls went to different regions depending on their lives and deaths.

The Asphodel Meadows were where most souls ended up. This was the default afterlife for ordinary people who were neither particularly good nor particularly bad. The meadows were grey, dim, and boring. Souls wandered as shades, pale copies of their former selves. They had no strength, no passion, and no real existence. They recognized each other but could barely interact. It wasn't torture, but it wasn't pleasant either. It was existence without life, consciousness without vitality.

When Odysseus visited the underworld in the *Odyssey*, he encountered the shade of Achilles. Achilles, the greatest hero of the Trojan War, told him, "I would rather be a living slave to a poor man than king of all the dead." This was the Greek view of death. Even the most glorious afterlife was worse than the worst mortal existence.

Tartarus was the pit of punishment, as far below Hades as the earth was below the sky. An anvil dropped from Earth would fall for nine days before hitting Tartarus. This was where the worst offenders went, those who had committed crimes against the gods or violated the fundamental cosmic order.

Tartarus was surrounded by the River Phlegethon and triple walls of bronze. Inside, the Titans who had fought Zeus remained imprisoned, guarded by the Hecatoncheires. Human souls sent to Tartarus faced eternal, creative punishments designed to fit their crimes. We'll explore some of these punishments shortly.

The Elysian Fields, or Elysium, were paradise. Only the greatest heroes, those favored by the gods, or those related to divine bloodlines went there. Elysium was beautiful. It had an eternal spring, gentle breezes, comfortable temperatures, and abundant food. Heroes could feast, compete in games, enjoy music, and live in comfort forever.

Some sources placed Elysium at the edge of the world rather than in the underworld. It was known as the Isles of the Blessed, where chosen souls lived in perfect happiness away from both the living and the ordinary dead.

Later Greek philosophy introduced the idea that souls in Elysium could choose to be reincarnated. If a soul lived three virtuous lives and returned to Elysium three times, they would be sent to the ultimate paradise, the Islands of the Blessed, and remain there forever. This belief was particularly associated with Orphic mystery cults and philosophers like Plato rather than mainstream Greek religion.

Later writers, especially the Romans, added more specific regions to the underworld's geography. The Fields of Mourning, popularized by Virgil in the *Aeneid*, were where those who died from love went. Souls who committed suicide for love or died of heartbreak wandered here, forever experiencing the pain that killed them. Dido, the Carthaginian queen who killed herself when Aeneas abandoned her, ended up here in Virgil's telling.

The Judges

Three judges decided where souls went: Minos, Rhadamanthus, and Aeacus. All three had been exceptionally just kings during their mortal lives. When they died, Hades appointed them as judges of the dead.

Minos, the famous king of Crete who had commissioned the Labyrinth, was often portrayed as the chief judge. During his life, he had been so just that Zeus himself gave him laws. Every nine years, Minos would ascend to a cave on Mount Ida to receive new laws directly from Zeus. His reputation for wisdom and fairness made him the principal judge in the underworld.

Rhadamanthus, Minos's brother, was known for his stern inflexibility. He never bent rules, never showed favoritism, and never allowed excuses. Some sources say he specifically judged the souls sent to the Elysian Fields, determining who was worthy of paradise.

Aeacus, grandfather of Achilles, was famous for his piety and justice. During his mortal reign on Aegina, he was so beloved by the gods that when a plague depopulated his island, Zeus transformed ants into people to give him new subjects. His reputation for fairness earned him a role among the judges.

The three judges sat at a crossroads in the underworld where the paths diverged. Later sources, particularly Plato's *Gorgias*, organized their duties geographically: Minos judged Europeans, Rhadamanthus judged Asians, and Aeacus judged islanders, though earlier sources were less specific about this division.

But the judgment wasn't based on universal moral goodness. The Greeks didn't have a concept of sin as later religions defined it. Instead, the judges looked for specific violations of *themis* (cosmic order and sacred law).

Orpheus and Eurydice:
The Most Tragic Love Song in History

Orpheus is perhaps the most famous for trying to win a soul back from death. While other myths feature resurrections, Alcestis was brought back when Heracles wrestled Death itself, and various heroes were restored by divine intervention, Orpheus attempted something unique: to move the unmovable lords of the dead through the power of music and love. His story is the ultimate tale of that attempt and its heartbreaking failure.

The Greatest Musician

Orpheus was the son of Apollo (or of a mortal king, depending on the source) and the Muse Calliope. He inherited supernatural musical ability. When Orpheus played his lyre and sang, animals stopped to listen. Trees bent toward him. Rivers changed course to hear his music. Rocks wept. Even the gods paused to listen.

Orpheus joined Jason and the Argonauts on their quest for the Golden Fleece. When the Argonauts passed the Sirens, Orpheus played music so beautiful it drowned out the Sirens' song. He saved the entire crew.

When Orpheus returned from his adventures, he fell in love with a nymph named Eurydice. They married, and Orpheus was happier than he'd ever been. His music became even more beautiful, filled with joy and love.

Nymphs Listening to the Songs of Orpheus *by Charles François Jalabert.*[20]

On their wedding day, or shortly after, depending on the version, Eurydice was walking through a meadow with her fellow nymphs. She caught the eye of Aristaeus, a minor god and beekeeper, who pursued her with unwelcome romantic intentions.

Eurydice fled. In her haste to escape, she stepped on a snake hidden in the grass. The snake bit her. The venom was deadly. Within moments, Eurydice collapsed and died.

Orpheus was devastated. He sang songs of such profound grief that all of nature mourned with him. Trees shed their leaves out of season. Rivers overflowed with sympathetic tears. His music was so sad that even the gods wept.

But mourning wasn't enough. Orpheus couldn't accept Eurydice's death. He made a decision that was either incredibly brave or incredibly foolish. He would go to the underworld and bring her back.

Living people didn't enter Hades. It was forbidden. But Orpheus found an entrance, a cave that led downward into the earth, and descended anyway.

He brought only his lyre. His plan was simple. He would charm the lords of the dead with music so beautiful they couldn't refuse him.

He crossed the River Styx. Charon, the ferryman, was so moved by Orpheus's grief-stricken songs that he ferried him across without demanding payment. Cerberus, the three-headed guardian, lay down and let Orpheus pass, all three heads lulled by the music.

The shades of the dead gathered to listen. They remembered what it was like to feel emotions. They remembered being alive. Orpheus's music gave them a momentary glimpse of the life they'd lost.

The judges paused their work. The punishments in Tartarus stopped. Sisyphus sat on his boulder. Tantalus forgot his hunger and thirst. The Danaids rested from their endless water-carrying. Everyone in the underworld stopped to listen.

Finally, Orpheus reached the throne room of Hades and Persephone. He stood before the king and queen of the dead and played. He sang of his love for Eurydice, of their short happiness, of his unbearable grief. He sang of the cruelty of death that took her so young. He asked, begged, for one exception to the eternal rule. Let Eurydice return to life. Let them grow old together. Let her die naturally when her time came, and then he would never ask again.

Persephone, who understood being taken from the world above, wept openly. Even Hades was moved. For the first and only time, Hades granted mercy.

"You may take Eurydice back," Hades said. "But there is one condition. She will follow you. You cannot look back at her until you both reach the surface and see sunlight. If you turn around before then, even once, she will return to the dead forever. Do you accept?"

Orpheus accepted immediately. The condition seemed easy. Just walk forward and don't look back. He could do that.

Eurydice's shade was brought to him. She was pale and limping from the snake bite. But she was there. She was his.

They began the long journey back to the surface.

Orpheus led the way. Eurydice followed behind him. He couldn't see her and couldn't hear her footsteps since shades made no sound. He could only trust that she was there.

They climbed through the darkness. Past Tartarus. Past the judges. Past the River Styx. The path was long and steep. Orpheus wanted desperately to turn around, to make sure Eurydice was still following, to see her face one more time. But he didn't. He kept walking.

They approached the entrance. Orpheus could see light ahead, the blessed, beautiful light of the surface world. He was almost there. Just a few more steps.

Different versions give different reasons for what happened next.

In some versions, Orpheus reached the surface and stepped into the sunlight. Believing he'd satisfied the condition, he turned around to embrace Eurydice. But she was still in shadow, one step behind. She hadn't yet reached the surface.

In other versions, Orpheus heard a sound behind him, maybe Eurydice stumbling, maybe a cry, and turned around in fear that she'd fallen or was in danger.

In the most tragic version, Orpheus simply doubted. He thought, "What if Hades tricked me? What if she's not really there? What if I'm climbing alone?" The doubt grew unbearable. Just before reaching the surface, unable to trust, he turned around to check.

Eurydice was there. She'd been there the whole time, following faithfully. Their eyes met. Orpheus saw relief and love in her face.

But then she began to fade. She reached out to him, but her hand passed through his like mist. She tried to speak, but no sound came. She was pulled backward, down into the darkness, becoming less substantial with each moment.

"Farewell," she whispered, or maybe Orpheus only imagined it. Then she was gone.

Orpheus tried to follow her back down, but this time, Charon refused to ferry him. The dead couldn't return to life, and the living were only allowed one journey to the underworld. Orpheus had used his chance.

He returned to the surface alone. He never loved again. Orpheus spent his remaining years playing mournful music, rejecting all romantic advances. Some sources say he swore off women entirely and only kept company with young men.

His rejection of women's affection angered the Maenads, the female followers of Dionysus. During one of their frenzied rituals, they tore Orpheus limb from limb. They threw his severed head and his lyre into a river. The head floated downstream, still singing, until it reached the sea. The lyre was placed in the sky as the constellation Lyra.

Even in death, Orpheus and Eurydice were reunited. His shade descended to the underworld, and this time, he was allowed to stay. He found Eurydice's shade in the Asphodel Meadows. They walked together forever, and now, finally, he could look at her all he wanted.

The story is heartbreaking because Orpheus almost succeeded. He did the impossible. He had charmed Hades himself. All he had to do was trust and walk forward. And he couldn't do it.

The myth teaches something painful. Love isn't always enough. Good intentions don't guarantee success. Sometimes you can do everything right and still fail because you're human and humans are flawed.

Other Descents to the Underworld

Orpheus wasn't the only living person to descend to Hades's realm. Several heroes made the journey and returned, each for different reasons and with different outcomes.

Theseus and Pirithous attempted a descent with catastrophic results. Pirithous wanted to kidnap Persephone to be his wife. Theseus, bound by friendship, agreed to help despite knowing it was insane. Hades pretended to welcome them, invited them to sit, and trapped them in the chairs of forgetfulness. They sat there for years until Heracles freed Theseus during his own descent. Pirithous remained trapped forever. His presumption had been too great to forgive.

Heracles descended for his twelfth labor to capture Cerberus. Unlike Orpheus, Heracles used force rather than music. He wrestled the three-headed dog into submission with his bare hands, brought it to the surface to show King Eurystheus, and then returned it to its post. During his time below, Heracles also freed Theseus, who had been trapped there after foolishly trying to kidnap Persephone.

Odysseus visited the underworld in Homer's *Odyssey*, though he didn't actually enter it. He performed rituals at the entrance that summoned the shades to him. He spoke with his dead mother, consulted the prophet Tiresias, and encountered the shades of famous heroes, including Achilles and Agamemnon. This visit, called a *nekyia* (summoning of the dead), showed him the grim reality of death and reinforced his desire to return home.

Aeneas, in Virgil's later Roman epic, descended to the underworld guided by the Sibyl of Cumae. He carried a golden bough that granted him safe passage. There, he met his father, Anchises, who showed him the future glories of Rome and explained the cycle of reincarnation. This *katabasis* (descent) was modeled on Odysseus's but had Roman philosophical and political meaning.

The Eternal Punishments:
Sisyphus, Tantalus, and the Danaids

Tartarus wasn't just a prison. It was a place of eternal torment for those who'd committed the worst crimes. The punishments were designed to fit the crimes.

Three punishments became especially famous, each teaching a different lesson about what happens when you violate the cosmic order.

Sisyphus: The Clever King Who Outsmarted Death

Sisyphus was the king of Corinth. He was known for being the cleverest and most cunning mortal who ever lived. He was also ruthless, greedy, and willing to betray anyone for personal gain.

His crimes formed a pattern of betrayal that deeply offended the gods. He murdered travelers and guests, violating the sacred laws of hospitality protected by Zeus. He seduced his niece. Most seriously, he repeatedly betrayed Zeus himself through a series of escalating offenses.

When Zeus abducted the river nymph Aegina, her father Asopus searched everywhere for her. Sisyphus knew where she was—Zeus had hidden her on an island. Sisyphus made a deal. If Asopus created a freshwater spring for Corinth, which desperately needed water, Sisyphus would reveal Zeus's hiding place.

Asopus agreed and created the spring Peirene. Sisyphus betrayed Zeus's secret. Zeus was furious. Sisyphus had traded divine secrets for civic infrastructure, showing no respect for the king of the gods. Zeus sent

Thanatos, Death personified, to drag Sisyphus to the underworld immediately.

But Sisyphus was clever. When Thanatos arrived with chains to bind him, Sisyphus asked innocently, "How do these chains work? Can you show me?" Thanatos, proud of his equipment, demonstrated. Sisyphus immediately locked Thanatos in the chains.

With Death imprisoned, no one could die. Warriors fought battles where everyone was wounded, but no one died. Old people grew older and more decrepit, but they couldn't pass away. The natural order was breaking down.

Finally, Ares, who missed the carnage of war where people actually died, freed Thanatos. Death came for Sisyphus again.

But Sisyphus had prepared one more trick. He told his wife not to perform burial rites for him. When he arrived in the underworld, he complained to Persephone that his wife had disrespected him by leaving him unburied. He begged permission to return to the surface briefly to scold her and ensure proper burial rites.

Persephone was sympathetic, so she allowed it. Sisyphus returned to life.

And stayed there. He had no intention of going back. He lived for many more years, laughing at having tricked Death twice.

Eventually, Sisyphus died naturally from old age. This time, there was no escape. Hades personally dragged him to Tartarus and assigned his punishment.

Sisyphus was condemned to roll a massive boulder up a steep hill. When he reached the top, the boulder would roll back down, and he had to start over. For all eternity, he would push that rock up the hill, almost succeed, and watch it roll back down.

Sisyphus had tried to cheat Death, to halt its progress entirely. Now he was condemned to endless progress without purpose. Any achievement would be forever out of reach.

Sisyphus by Titian.[21]

Tantalus: The King Who Served His Son to the Gods

Tantalus was the king of Lydia and the son of Zeus himself. He was wealthy beyond measure and privileged to dine with the gods on Olympus. The gods trusted him.

He betrayed that trust in the worst possible way.

Tantalus committed several crimes. Sources vary on which was worse. He stole nectar and ambrosia from the gods' table and shared it with mortals, trying to make them immortal. He revealed divine secrets to humans. However, his most horrific crime involved his own son, Pelops.

Tantalus invited the gods to a feast at his palace. The gods accepted, honoring him with their presence. Tantalus wanted to test whether the gods were truly omniscient, whether they really knew everything. So he killed his son Pelops, butchered the body, cooked the flesh, and served it to the gods as the main course.

The gods immediately recognized what they were being served. All of them refused to eat, except Demeter, who was distracted by grief over Persephone's abduction and absently ate part of Pelops's shoulder before realizing what it was.

The gods were horrified and furious. They brought Pelops back to life, replacing his missing shoulder with one made of ivory, and turned their full wrath on Tantalus.

Zeus cast Tantalus into Tartarus with a punishment that would last forever.

Tantalus stood in a pool of water up to his chin. Above his head hung branches laden with ripe fruit, apples, pears, and figs, all within easy reach. He was desperately hungry and thirsty, having eaten nothing and drunk nothing since his death.

He bent his head to drink. The water immediately receded, sinking until it was just out of reach. When he stood upright, the water returned to chin level.

He reached for the fruit. The wind blew the branches just out of reach. When he stopped reaching, the branches swung back to where they'd been.

He stood in water he couldn't drink, beneath food he couldn't eat, experiencing hunger and thirst with relief always one inch away. The word "tantalize" comes from his name, meaning to tempt with something you can never have.

The Danaids: The Brides Who Murdered Their Husbands

The fifty daughters of King Danaus were known as the Danaids. Their father was in a power struggle with his brother Aegyptus, who had fifty sons. To end the feud, Aegyptus proposed that his fifty sons marry Danaus's fifty daughters, uniting the families.

Danaus didn't trust his brother. He agreed to the marriages but secretly commanded his daughters to kill their husbands on their wedding night.

Forty-nine of the fifty daughters obeyed. On their wedding night, they murdered their new husbands in their beds. Only one daughter,

Hypermnestra, refused. She loved her husband, Lynceus, and couldn't kill him. She helped him escape instead.

The forty-nine who committed murder eventually died and were sent to Tartarus for violating the sacred bond of marriage on the very night it was formed.

Their punishment was elegant in its futility. They had to fill a large jar, or bathtub, depending on the version, with water. They were given buckets and sent to a well. They filled their buckets, carried them back, and poured the water into the jar.

But the jar had holes in the bottom. The water drained out as fast as they poured it in. They could never fill it. It was an endless, pointless task.

Ixion: The Burning Wheel

Ixion was the king of the Lapiths who committed multiple terrible crimes. First, he murdered his father-in-law by pushing him into a pit of burning coals to avoid paying the bride-price he'd promised. This was the first murder of a blood relative in Greek mythology, making it an unprecedented crime.

The other gods shunned him for this violation, but Zeus took pity and purified him of the murder. Zeus even invited Ixion to dine on Olympus, an extraordinary honor for a mortal.

Ixion repaid this divine kindness by trying to seduce Hera, Zeus's wife.

Zeus, suspecting Ixion's intentions, created a cloud named Nephele in Hera's exact form to test him. Ixion was completely fooled and had relations with the cloud-Hera. From this union was born Centaurus, the ancestor of the centaurs, which explains why centaurs in mythology were often portrayed as lustful and prone to violence.

Zeus was furious. He had shown Ixion unprecedented mercy and hospitality, and Ixion had responded by attempting to assault the queen of the gods. The punishment had to match the audacity of the crime.

Ixion was bound to a fiery wheel that spun through the underworld (or the sky, in some versions) for all eternity. The wheel was wreathed in flames and never stopped turning. Ixion experienced perpetual burning, dizziness, and pain with no possibility of rest or relief.

Some sources say Zeus made the wheel visible in the sky as a warning to all mortals.

Tityos: The Vultures' Feast

Tityos was a Giant, described as being so large that he covered nine acres when lying down. He was a son of Zeus or Gaia, sources disagree, which made his crime even more offensive to the divine order.

Tityos attempted to rape Leto, the mother of Apollo and Artemis. Some versions say Hera put him up to it, jealous of yet another of Zeus's lovers. Others say Tityos acted on his own lustful impulses.

Apollo and Artemis defended their mother and shot Tityos with arrows, killing him. But death was only the beginning of his punishment.

In Tartarus, Tityos was stretched out over an enormous expanse of ground. Two vultures descended on him daily to eat his liver. Every night, the liver regenerated. Every day, the birds returned to feast again.

This punishment parallels Prometheus's torment, but there is a crucial difference. Prometheus suffered for helping humanity and was eventually freed by Heracles. Tityos suffered for attempted rape and would never be freed. The Greeks drew a sharp distinction between noble suffering and deserved eternal torment.

When Odysseus visited the underworld in the *Odyssey*, he witnessed Tityos sprawled across the ground with vultures tearing at his organs.

Chapter 7: The Trojan War

The Trojan War was the defining event of Greek mythology. It brought together all the greatest heroes of the age, involved nearly every god on Olympus, lasted ten years, and ended with the complete destruction of one of the most powerful cities in the ancient world.

But it started because of an apple.

Well, technically, it started because of a beauty contest. Or a kidnapping. Or maybe it was inevitable from the moment the gods decided to meddle in human affairs. The causes of the Trojan War stacked up like dominoes, with each event triggering the next until war became unavoidable.

The Apple of Discord:
How a Wedding Caused a War

Every disaster has a beginning. The Trojan War's beginning was a wedding that one goddess wasn't invited to.

Peleus was a mortal hero, a veteran of the Argonauts' quest for the Golden Fleece. Thetis was a sea nymph, one of the Nereids, daughters of the sea god Nereus. She was extraordinarily beautiful, and both Zeus and Poseidon wanted to marry her.

But there was a prophecy. Thetis would bear a son greater than his father. If Zeus married her, their son would overthrow him, just as Zeus had overthrown Cronus. The gods couldn't allow this.

So, Zeus arranged for Thetis to marry a mortal instead. Her son would be greater than his mortal father, but he would be no threat to the gods. Thetis hated this. She was a goddess forced to marry a human, doomed to watch her husband age and die while she remained eternally young.

But she had no choice. The wedding was arranged. All the gods and goddesses were invited to attend. It was a major event. Mortals rarely married immortals, and this marriage had cosmic significance.

All the gods were invited.

Well, all except one.

Eris, goddess of discord and strife, was deliberately excluded. She caused trouble wherever she went. She fed on conflict and chaos. The gods decided the wedding would be more pleasant without her.

Eris was furious. If they wanted to exclude her, fine. She'd give them discord anyway.

She appeared at the wedding feast uninvited. She threw a golden apple onto the table among the guests. On the apple was inscribed, "For the Fairest."

Then she left.

Three goddesses immediately claimed the apple. Hera, Athena, and Aphrodite each insisted she was the fairest and deserved the prize.

The other gods wisely refused to judge. Choosing one goddess would make enemies of the other two. Zeus, who wasn't stupid, delegated the decision. He told Hermes to take the three goddesses to Mount Ida, near Troy, where a young prince named Paris was tending sheep. Paris would judge which goddess was fairest.

Paris was the son of King Priam and Queen Hecuba of Troy, but he'd been abandoned as an infant. An oracle had prophesied that Paris would bring about Troy's destruction, so Priam ordered him to be left on Mount Ida to die. But shepherds found him and raised him as their own. He grew up as a shepherd, unaware of his royal heritage, and was known for his beauty and supposed fairness in judgment.

The Judgement of Paris *by Enrique Simonet.*[22]

The three goddesses appeared before Paris. Each knew that beauty alone might not be enough to win, so they offered bribes.

Hera promised power. If Paris chose her, she would make him ruler of all of Europe and Asia. He would be the most powerful king who ever lived.

Athena promised glory in war. If Paris chose her, she would make him the greatest warrior, victorious in every battle, and famous throughout history.

Aphrodite promised love. If Paris chose her, she would give him the most beautiful woman in the world as his wife.

Paris, young and foolish and thinking with something other than his brain, chose Aphrodite.

So, Aphrodite won the golden apple. Hera and Athena became her eternal enemies and swore to destroy Troy. This single decision set everything else in motion.

Helen of Sparta

The most beautiful woman in the world was Helen, daughter of Zeus and Leda. Helen's beauty was so extraordinary that every prince in Greece wanted to marry her. Her mortal father, King Tyndareus of Sparta, faced a problem. When he chose a husband for Helen, all the rejected suitors might attack him or each other out of jealousy.

Odysseus, one of the suitors, suggested a solution. Make all the suitors swear an oath. They would accept Helen's choice, and they would defend her chosen husband against anyone who tried to take her. All the suitors swore this oath.

Helen chose Menelaus, brother of Agamemnon and king of Sparta. They married and had a daughter, Hermione.

Then Paris came to Sparta.

Paris had learned his true identity and been welcomed back to Troy as a prince. King Priam sent him on a diplomatic mission to Greece. Paris visited Menelaus in Sparta and was welcomed with full hospitality, one of the most sacred bonds in Greek culture.

What happened next depends on who's telling the story. Did Paris abduct Helen by force? Did she willingly run away with him, bored with her marriage? Was she under Aphrodite's spell, unable to resist? Different ancient sources give different answers. Some paint Helen as a victim with no choice. Others suggest she was looking for adventure. Still others say Aphrodite's magic made the decision for her. The Greeks themselves never agreed on whether Helen was innocent or guilty.

Regardless, Paris and Helen sailed back to Troy, taking much of Sparta's treasury with them.

When Menelaus returned and discovered his wife and wealth were gone, he was enraged. He called on his brother Agamemnon, the most powerful king in Greece, for help. Agamemnon reminded all of Helen's former suitors of their oath.

The kings of Greece had no choice. They'd sworn by the gods. Breaking such an oath would bring divine wrath. They gathered their armies and prepared for war.

The Sacrifice at Aulis

The Greek fleet assembled at Aulis, a harbor on the coast of Boeotia. Over a thousand ships gathered there, carrying tens of thousands of warriors. It was the largest military expedition Greece had ever seen.

But they couldn't sail. Day after day, the winds blew from the wrong direction, keeping the fleet trapped in the harbor. Weeks passed. The army grew restless. Supplies dwindled, and men began deserting.

The prophet Calchas revealed the cause. Artemis was angry. Agamemnon had killed a deer in one of her sacred groves and boasted that he was a better hunter than the goddess. Artemis demanded payment for this hubris.

The price was Agamemnon's daughter, Iphigenia. She had to be sacrificed to Artemis before the fleet could sail.

Agamemnon faced an impossible choice. Refuse, and the war would end before it began. The army would disband. He'd be dishonored, having gathered all of Greece for nothing. Accept, and he'd have to murder his own daughter.

He chose the war.

Agamemnon sent word to his wife, Clytemnestra. Bring Iphigenia to Aulis. He claimed she was to marry Achilles. Clytemnestra, believing this was a wedding, brought their daughter eagerly.

When they arrived, though, Iphigenia learned the truth. Different versions tell what happened next. In some, she accepted her fate nobly, choosing to die so Greece could sail. In others, she was dragged screaming to the altar.

The Sacrifice of Iphigenia *by Charles de La Fosse.*[28]

In some tellings, Artemis took pity at the last second and substituted a deer on the altar, spiriting Iphigenia away to serve as her priestess in distant Tauris. Iphigenia lived, though her family believed her dead. In other versions, Artemis didn't intervene. Agamemnon killed his daughter. Her blood soaked the altar, and the winds changed.

Either way, Clytemnestra never forgave her husband. She would wait years for his return from Troy. And while she waited, she planned her revenge.

The fleet sailed for Troy, carried on winds purchased with innocent blood.

The Major Players:
Achilles, Hector, Ajax, and Odysseus

The Trojan War brought together the greatest heroes of the age. On both sides, men fought for honor, glory, and survival. These are the warriors who defined the conflict.

Achilles: The Best of the Greeks

Achilles was the son of Peleus and Thetis, the same wedding that started all the trouble. He was the grandson of Aeacus, great-grandson of Zeus, and half-divine through his mother. He was the greatest warrior who ever lived.

Thetis knew from prophecy that Achilles had two possible fates. He could live a long, peaceful life in obscurity, or he could die young at Troy and achieve eternal glory. She tried to prevent him from going to war.

In one version, she disguised him as a girl and hid him among the daughters of King Lycomedes on the island of Scyros. Odysseus, knowing the Greeks couldn't win without Achilles, came to the island posing as a merchant. He spread out goods for the girls to examine. There was jewelry, fine cloth, and, hidden among them, weapons. While the girls looked at the pretty things, Achilles instinctively grabbed the weapons. His cover was blown.

Achilles joined the war on the side of the Greeks. He knew it would kill him, but he chose glory over a long life. He brought fifty ships and his Myrmidons, elite warriors from his homeland of Phthia who fought under his command with legendary discipline and ferocity.

Achilles was nearly invincible in battle. According to legend, his mother Thetis had dipped him in the River Styx as an infant, making him

invulnerable everywhere except the heel she held him by. This famous
"Achilles heel" story is actually a later addition. It doesn't appear in the
original Greek epics. In the *Iliad*, Achilles is simply the best warrior
through natural talent and divine parentage. His armor was forged by
Hephaestus himself. His rage in battle was terrifying. No one could stand
against him.

Thetis dipping the infant Achilles into the river Styx *by Peter Paul Rubens.*[34]

However, Achilles had a massive flaw: his pride. He demanded honor
and respect above all else. When that honor was challenged, his rage
could destroy everything around him, including his own side.

Hector: Defender of Troy

Hector was Paris's older brother, the crown prince of Troy and its greatest warrior. He was everything Paris wasn't. He was brave, honorable, responsible, and beloved by his people.

Hector didn't want the war. He knew Paris had dishonored the laws of hospitality by taking Helen, and he knew Troy would suffer for his brother's actions. But Troy was his city, his family's home, and his responsibility. When the Greeks came for revenge, Hector put on his armor and fought.

Hector was a devoted husband to Andromache and a loving father to his infant son, Astyanax. He was a loyal brother, even to the foolish Paris. He fought not for glory or pride but because it was his duty to protect his home.

The most famous scene in the *Iliad* shows Hector saying goodbye to his family before battle. He removes his helmet because it frightens his baby son. He holds the child and prays to the gods that his son will grow up to be a great warrior who will make his mother proud. He knows he might not return. But he goes anyway because that's what heroes do.

As long as Hector lived, the city held. He killed more Greeks than any other Trojan. He was brave, skilled, and commanded respect from both sides.

But he couldn't stand against Achilles.

Ajax (The Greater): The Massive Warrior

There were two warriors named Ajax at Troy. Ajax the Greater, son of Telamon, was massive. He was a giant of a man, second only to Achilles in combat prowess. He carried an enormous shield made of seven layers of ox hide covered in bronze. He was strong enough to wield this shield and still fight effectively.

Ajax was reliable. He was steady. He didn't have Achilles's brilliance or Odysseus's cunning, but he was always there, always fighting, always holding the line. When Achilles refused to fight, which we'll get to, Ajax became the Greeks' main defense against Hector.

Ajax saved the Greek ships from being burned. He fought Hector to a draw in single combat. He was the rock the Greek army depended on.

After the war, Ajax and Odysseus both claimed Achilles's armor as a prize. The Greeks voted, and Odysseus won. Ajax, feeling dishonored, went mad. In his madness, he slaughtered a flock of sheep, thinking they were his enemies. When his sanity returned, and he realized what he'd done, he was so ashamed that he killed himself. Even the greatest heroes could be destroyed by wounded pride.

Odysseus: The Cunning King

Odysseus, king of Ithaca, didn't want to go to Troy. He'd just married Penelope and had a newborn son, Telemachus. When recruiters came to draft him for the war, Odysseus pretended to be insane, plowing his fields with an ox and a donkey yoked together and sowing salt instead of seed.

But Palamedes, one of the recruiters, suspected Odysseus was faking. He placed baby Telemachus in front of the plow. Odysseus immediately stopped. A madman wouldn't have cared about running over a child. Odysseus had to join the war. He never forgave Palamedes for this trick and later arranged his death. Odysseus forged a letter supposedly from Priam, king of Troy, and planted gold in Palamedes's tent. The forged letter made it appear that Palamedes was a traitor working with the enemy. The Greeks were outraged. Palamedes was executed by stoning.

Odysseus wasn't the best warrior, but he was clever. He was the strategist, the schemer, the one who solved problems that couldn't be solved with a sword. He was good with words, good at manipulation, and good at thinking ten steps ahead.

The Greeks respected strength, but they also valued cunning (*metis* in Greek). When brute force failed, Odysseus found another way. When the war reached a stalemate, Odysseus would be the one to end it, not with strength but with a trick.

Others Worth Knowing

Agamemnon was the commander of the Greek forces. He was the king of Mycenae and Menelaus's brother. He was powerful, proud, and not particularly likable. His quarrel with Achilles nearly cost the Greeks the war.

Menelaus, Helen's husband, was the reason for the war, but he was not its greatest warrior. He was competent but was overshadowed by his brother and the other heroes.

Diomedes was one of the younger Greek warriors and one of the most effective. In one battle, with Athena's help, he even wounded Ares and Aphrodite. The gods feared him.

Paris was the cause of the war, but he was not much of a warrior. He was an archer, which the Greeks considered less honorable than face-to-face combat with a sword or spear. He killed Achilles with an arrow but otherwise contributed little to Troy's defense.

Priam was the elderly king of Troy. He was father to fifty sons, including Hector and Paris. He was wise, but his life became tragic as he was forced to watch his city be destroyed because of one son's foolishness. His best son died trying to prevent it.

Andromache was Hector's wife and one of the most tragic figures in the war. She lost her husband and then watched the Greeks murder her infant son by throwing him from Troy's walls so he couldn't grow up to avenge his father.

These were the major players. The war would break some of them, kill others, and haunt the survivors for the rest of their lives.

The First Nine Years: Why It Took So Long

The *Iliad* begins in the tenth year of the war. What happened in the first nine?

The Greeks didn't attack Troy directly. The city was too well fortified and too well supplied. Troy had allies throughout the region who could provide reinforcements and resources. A direct siege would fail.

So, the Greeks adopted a different strategy. They spent years raiding and destroying Troy's allies and supply lines. They attacked the surrounding cities and islands, cutting off Troy's support network, capturing resources, and taking prisoners who could be ransomed or enslaved.

These raids weakened Troy's ability to resist. They also enriched the Greek warriors with plunder and kept the army occupied. Ten years is a long time to keep men away from home, and they needed both purpose and payment.

During these raids, the Greeks captured many women who became prizes and caused conflicts in the *Iliad*. Chryseis, whose capture triggered the plague, was taken in a raid. Briseis, the woman Agamemnon stole from Achilles, was captured when her city fell.

Achilles was particularly active in these campaigns. According to the *Iliad*, he personally sacked twelve cities by sea and eleven by land. In one raid, he killed King Eëtion and his seven sons, taking Andromache's family from her. These raids established Achilles's reputation as the Greeks' most effective warrior.

The strategy worked, but slowly. Troy was isolated but not broken. The city's walls remained impregnable. King Priam was wealthy and could sustain a siege. The Greeks controlled the surrounding territory but couldn't take the city itself.

Both sides settled into a grinding war of attrition. The Greeks built a fortified camp near the beach where they had pulled up their ships. The Trojans stayed behind their walls except when fighting. Battles were fought in the plain between the city and the Greek camp, with neither side able to achieve a decisive victory.

The war dragged on. Year after year, men died in skirmishes and raids. Supplies ran low. Morale suffered. Some Greeks wanted to give up and go home. But the oath bound them, and pride prevented retreat.

By the tenth year, when the *Iliad* begins, both sides were exhausted. The Greeks had lost countless men and spent a decade away from home. Troy had lost allies, territory, and many of its warriors. Neither side could win, but neither would surrender.

The *Iliad's* Main Events:
The Wrath of Achilles and the Death of Hector

The *Iliad* focuses on a few weeks in the tenth year during a crisis caused by Achilles's wounded pride. But those weeks decided everything.

The Plague and the Quarrel

The *Iliad* opens with a plague ravaging the Greek camp. The priest of Apollo, Chryses, had come to ransom his daughter Chryseis, who had been taken as a war prize by Agamemnon. Agamemnon refused to return her and insulted the priest.

Apollo, angered on behalf of his priest, sent a plague that killed Greeks by the hundreds. Finally, Achilles called an assembly to determine the cause. The prophet Calchas revealed the truth: Apollo was angry because Agamemnon had dishonored his priest. The plague would only end if Chryseis were returned.

Agamemnon agreed, but he was furious. He had been forced to give up his prize. To compensate, he demanded Achilles's prize, a woman named Briseis.

Achilles was outraged. He had won Briseis fairly in battle. Agamemnon was abusing his authority as commander to steal what was not his. This was a direct insult to Achilles's honor.

Achilles nearly killed Agamemnon on the spot, but Athena appeared—visible only to Achilles—and stopped him, promising that greater honor would come if he restrained himself. Achilles backed down, but he swore that he would no longer fight for the Greeks. Let them see how much they needed him. Let them beg.

He withdrew to his tent with his closest companion, Patroclus. The Myrmidons withdrew from battle. The Greeks' best warrior sat idle while his comrades died.

Thetis, Achilles's mother, went to Zeus and begged him to honor her son. She asked Zeus to let the Trojans win battles and to push the Greeks to the brink of destruction so they would realize how much they needed Achilles and beg him to return.

Zeus agreed. He was already sympathetic to Troy—he had tried to prevent the war—and honoring Thetis cost him nothing. He sent a false dream to Agamemnon, suggesting the Greeks could win a quick victory, knowing it would fail.

The tide of war turned. With Achilles refusing to fight, Hector became unstoppable. He pushed the Greeks back toward their ships. He killed dozens of Greek warriors. At one point, he breached the Greek defensive wall and threatened to burn their ships. If the ships burned, the Greeks could not return home. They would be stranded and destroyed.

But the gods were also fighting. They had chosen sides in the war, and their interventions shaped every major battle.

The Divine Factions

Hera, Athena, and Poseidon supported the Greeks. Hera and Athena were still furious about losing the beauty contest, and Poseidon was angry over an old grudge with Troy. Aphrodite, Apollo, and Ares supported the Trojans—Aphrodite because Paris had chosen her, Apollo because he loved Troy's culture, and Ares because he loved war and followed Aphrodite.

Zeus tried to remain neutral. But he had promised Thetis to honor Achilles, which required letting the Trojans win temporarily.

The gods did not just watch; they also fought. When the Greek warrior Diomedes, aided by Athena, fought brilliantly, he encountered Aphrodite on the battlefield protecting her son Aeneas. Diomedes, emboldened by Athena, stabbed Aphrodite in the wrist. The goddess fled to Olympus, bleeding ichor (divine blood), crying to her mother Dione about being wounded by a mortal.

Then Diomedes faced Ares himself. With Athena guiding his spear, Diomedes wounded the god of war in the stomach. Ares screamed and fled to Olympus to complain to Zeus. Zeus was disgusted with his son, calling him the most hateful of all the gods, but healed him anyway.

At one point, Zeus forbade the gods from interfering. They ignored him. When Zeus was distracted—Hera seduced him to sleep so the Greeks could rally—Poseidon directly aided Greek warriors. Apollo responded by inspiring the Trojans. The gods clashed on the battlefield—Athena against Ares, Poseidon against Apollo—though most of these divine duels ended inconclusively. The gods could not truly harm one another.

This divine meddling frustrated both sides. Warriors never knew whether they were fighting only their opponents or also invisible divine forces. A warrior might be winning until a god turned the tide. The randomness of battle was explained by divine whim.

The Greeks were desperate. Odysseus, Diomedes, and other heroes fought brilliantly, but they could not replace Achilles. Ajax held the line, but he could not push Hector back.

Agamemnon sent ambassadors to Achilles, offering gifts, apologies, and even Briseis's return. Achilles refused. His honor had been damaged beyond repair. He would return to battle only if the Trojans threatened his own ships.

The Greeks continued to lose ground.

The Death of Patroclus

Patroclus was Achilles's closest companion. Their bond was intense and deep. He was the person Achilles loved most in the world. Some saw them as the ultimate warrior friendship, while others have depicted them as lovers. Either way, Patroclus was everything to Achilles.

Patroclus could not watch the Greeks suffer any longer while Achilles sulked. He went to Achilles and begged, "If you won't fight, at least let me lead the Myrmidons. Let me wear your armor. The Trojans will think you've returned, and they'll retreat."

Achilles agreed, but with strict conditions. "Drive the Trojans from the ships, then return. Do not pursue them to Troy's walls. Do not try to take glory that isn't yours."

Patroclus put on Achilles's armor and led the Myrmidons into battle. The Trojans, seeing Achilles's distinctive armor, panicked and retreated.

Patroclus drove them back from the ships. He killed dozens of Trojans.

But he did not stop. He ignored Achilles's warning. He pursued the Trojans toward their city walls, caught up in battle fury, believing he could accomplish what Achilles would have done.

Apollo himself intervened. The god appeared on the battlefield, struck Patroclus from behind, and dazed him. Patroclus's helmet fell off. His spear broke, and his armor loosened.

Hector saw his chance. He drove his spear through Patroclus's stomach. As Patroclus died, he prophesied, "You will not live long yourself. Achilles will kill you."

Hector stripped Achilles's armor from Patroclus's body and wore it himself. The Greeks barely recovered Patroclus's corpse after a brutal fight over his body.

The Wrath of Achilles

When Achilles learned Patroclus was dead, his grief was absolute. He screamed so loudly that his mother heard him from the depths of the sea. He tore his clothes, covered himself in ash, and wept.

Thetis came to him. She knew what would happen if Achilles returned to battle. The prophecy was clear that if Achilles killed Hector, Achilles himself would die soon after. She begged him not to fight.

Achilles did not care. Patroclus was dead. Hector had killed him. Nothing else mattered—not his own life, not glory, not even his mother's grief. He would kill Hector, and then he would accept whatever fate followed.

Thetis went to Hephaestus and commissioned new armor for her son. It was the most magnificent armor ever forged. Hephaestus created a shield decorated with all of human life: cities at peace and at war, farmers and shepherds, festivals and funerals, the ocean and the stars. The armor was divine, unbreakable, and radiant.

Achilles put on the armor and returned to battle transformed. He was no longer fighting for the Greeks or for honor. He was now a force of pure vengeance.

He slaughtered Trojans by the hundreds. He filled the River Scamander with so many corpses that the river itself rose up against him. He no longer cared about glory or honor. He wanted blood.

The Trojans retreated behind their walls—well, all except Hector.

The Duel

Hector knew he had to face Achilles. If he fled inside the walls, he would be called a coward. His honor demanded he stand and fight, even though he knew he would likely die.

King Priam and Queen Hecuba begged Hector to come inside the walls. Andromache, his wife, also pleaded with him. But Hector had killed Patroclus, and he knew he had to answer for it.

When Achilles approached, Hector's courage faltered. He ran. Three times, Achilles chased Hector around the walls of Troy while both armies watched. It was humiliating, but Hector could not make himself stop.

Finally, Athena intervened. She disguised herself as Hector's brother Deiphobus and appeared beside him, saying she would fight alongside him. Encouraged, Hector turned to face Achilles.

The two greatest warriors of their generation fought. Hector threw his spear. It bounced off the divine shield. He called for Deiphobus to give him another spear, but Deiphobus had vanished.

Hector realized he had been deceived. He faced Achilles alone. So, he drew his sword for a final stand.

Achilles studied Hector's armor—his own armor, taken from Patroclus's body. He knew every weak point. He drove his spear into the gap at Hector's collarbone. Hector fell, dying.

As he died, Hector begged, "Return my body to my father for proper burial. Let my family mourn me."

Achilles refused. "I wish I could eat your flesh raw. Your body will be food for dogs and birds."

Hector died. Achilles tied his body to his chariot and dragged it around the walls of Troy while Priam and Hecuba watched in horror. He brought the corpse back to the Greek camp and continued to dishonor it daily, dragging it around Patroclus's funeral mound.

The Triumph of Achilles by Franz von Matsch. [25]

The gods were disgusted. Dishonoring a corpse violated Greek values. Even enemies deserved a proper burial. Finally, Zeus ordered Achilles to return the body.

Priam's Ransom

In the most moving scene of the *Iliad*, the old king Priam came alone to Achilles's tent at night, guided by Hermes. He knelt before the man who had killed his son. He kissed Achilles's hands and begged him. "Think of your own father. He is old, like me. Someday, he will receive your body and mourn you. Honor that future grief. Return my son to me."

Achilles wept. He thought of his father, Peleus, whom he would never see again. He thought of Patroclus, whose loss had driven him to this revenge. He thought of Hector, who had also loved and been loved.

He returned Hector's body to Priam, and he granted a truce for the funeral. Priam brought his son home to Troy for proper rites.

The *Iliad* ends with Hector's funeral. Troy still stands. Achilles still lives. But both fates are sealed. Hector is dead. Achilles will die soon. Troy will fall.

The war is not over. But the outcome is no longer in doubt.

The Fall of Troy:
The Trojan Horse and the End of an Era

The story of Achilles's final battles and death comes from the *Aethiopis*, a now-lost poem from the Epic Cycle (a collection of ancient Greek poems), and later Roman-era sources like Quintus Smyrnaeus's *Posthomerica*.

After Hector's death, Achilles continued to fight brilliantly. He killed Penthesilea, queen of the Amazons, who'd come to aid Troy. As Penthesilea died, Achilles removed her helmet and saw her face. He fell in love with her in that moment, but it was too late. The Greek warrior Thersites mocked him for this, and Achilles killed him in rage.

He killed Memnon, king of Ethiopia and son of Eos (goddess of dawn), another ally of Troy. Memnon was nearly Achilles's equal. When Memnon fell, his mother Eos wept, and her tears became the morning dew.

However, Achilles's death was prophesied and inevitable. Multiple omens had warned him. His mother had told him he would die soon after killing Hector. Even the dying Hector himself had prophesied Achilles's death.

His death came not in a glorious duel, but through fate and treachery. Paris, the Trojan prince, shot the arrow, although he did not act alone. The god Apollo, angered by Achilles's desecration of his temple and priest, guided the arrow to its mark. The arrow struck Achilles in his heel—his one vulnerable spot—and killed him.

The greatest warrior of the age died from an arrow shot by the least worthy of Troy's warriors.

The Greeks fought over his body. Ajax and Odysseus retrieved it and held off the Trojans. Achilles was given a magnificent funeral with games in his honor. His ashes were mixed with Patroclus's in a golden urn.

The Prophecies That Sealed Troy's Fate

The war might have dragged on forever, but ancient prophecies revealed what had to be done for Troy to fall. The Greeks couldn't win by force alone; they had to track down sacred relics and bring certain heroes to the battlefield.

The Palladium: Troy possessed a wooden statue of Athena called the Palladium. It had supposedly fallen from heaven. As long as the Palladium remained in Troy, the city couldn't be conquered. Odysseus and Diomedes infiltrated Troy by night, found the Palladium, and stole it. With this sacred protection gone, Troy became vulnerable.

Neoptolemus: Another prophecy stated that Troy required Achilles's son to fight for the Greeks. Neoptolemus (also called Pyrrhus) was young. He'd been conceived just before Achilles left for Troy and raised by his grandfather. Odysseus recruited him. Neoptolemus was as fierce as his father but more brutal, lacking Achilles's moments of nobility. He would be the one to murder King Priam at an altar during the sack of Troy.

Philoctetes and Heracles's Bow: Philoctetes was one of the greatest archers, wielding Heracles's own bow and poison arrows. But early in the conflict, he'd been bitten by a snake on the island of Lemnos. The wound festered, smelled terrible, and wouldn't heal. His constant screaming disrupted the camp. The Greeks abandoned him on Lemnos and sailed on.

Ten years later, they learned from a prophecy that Troy couldn't fall without Heracles's bow. Odysseus and Neoptolemus (Achilles's son) returned to Lemnos. They found Philoctetes still alive. He was still suffering and consumed with hatred for those who'd abandoned him. They convinced him to return. A healer cured his wound, and Philoctetes killed Paris with a poison arrow.

The Trojan Horse

Ten years of war, and Troy still stood. The walls were impregnable; they had been built by Poseidon and Apollo themselves in an earlier age. The city was well supplied from inland trade routes. Direct assault had failed repeatedly. The Greeks couldn't win by siege or force.

Odysseus proposed a trick that seemed insane but just might work.

The Greeks would build a massive wooden horse. It would be hollow inside and large enough to hold a certain number of warriors. They'd present it as an offering to Athena, asking for safe passage home, then sail away. The entire army would appear to give up and leave.

The Trojans, thinking they'd won, would drag the horse inside as a trophy. That night, the warriors hidden inside would emerge, kill the guards, and open Troy's gates. The Greek army, which would have only sailed out of sight to the nearby island of Tenedos, would return under the cover of darkness and pour into the undefended city.

The plan required everything to go perfectly. The Trojans had to take the bait, the hidden Greeks had to stay absolutely silent for hours cramped inside the horse, and the army had to return at exactly the right moment. It was absurd. It shouldn't work.

But they were desperate, and Odysseus was persuasive. So, they built the horse.

The craftsman Epeius designed it and supervised its construction. It was enormous, large enough to hold thirty to fifty warriors. The best and cleverest fighters volunteered: Odysseus, Diomedes, Menelaus, Neoptolemus, and others.

The rest of the Greek army packed up their camp, burned what they couldn't carry, boarded their ships, and sailed away toward the horizon. They left one man behind: Sinon, a Greek warrior chosen for his ability to lie convincingly. His job was to sell the deception.

When the Trojans woke up and saw the Greek camp had been abandoned, they couldn't believe it. Scouts confirmed it; the Greeks were gone. Only the massive wooden horse remained outside the gates.

The Trojans poured out of the city, celebrating. For the first time in ten years, they could walk freely in the plain that had been a battlefield. They explored the abandoned Greek camp, looking for anything useful left behind. Children played where soldiers had died.

But what about the horse?

Troy's citizens gathered around it, debating. Some wanted to drag it inside the city. Others wanted to burn it or push it off a cliff. The debate grew heated.

Trojan guards found Sinon hiding nearby, apparently trying to avoid capture. They dragged him before King Priam. Sinon told them that the Greeks had given up. Their morale had been broken, and their supplies were exhausted. They wanted to sail home. But the prophet Calchas said Athena demanded a human sacrifice to grant them safe passage.

Calchas chose Sinon. Odysseus and others bound him and prepared the sacrifice. However, the night before the ritual, Sinon escaped. The Greeks, in their hurry to leave before more bad omens appeared, sailed without him.

The horse was an offering to Athena. They'd offended her grievously during the war by stealing the Palladium and violating her temples. This offering was meant to regain her favor. They deliberately built it large so that the Trojans couldn't bring it into their walls. If the Trojans destroyed it, Athena would curse Troy. If they managed to bring it inside, Athena would bless Troy and curse the Greeks.

It was a masterful performance. Sinon even let himself be tortured to make the story convincing. He showed them marks where he'd supposedly been bound for sacrifice.

The Trojans debated whether to believe him. The priest Laocoön didn't believe any of it. He shouted, "I fear Greeks even bearing gifts!" He threw his spear at the horse, and it stuck in its wooden side with a hollow thud. If the Trojans had investigated the horse more closely at that moment, they would have heard the warriors inside and discovered the trick.

But then disaster struck. Two massive sea serpents emerged from the water and slithered toward the city. They attacked Laocoön and his two young sons, wrapping, strangling, and biting them. Laocoön and his sons died in agony while the horrified Trojans watched. The serpents then slithered to Athena's temple and coiled around the statue's base.

The Trojans interpreted this as divine judgment. Laocoön had been punished for throwing a spear at Athena's offering. The gods wanted the horse brought into Troy. Anyone who spoke against it might face similar divine wrath.

Cassandra, King Priam's daughter, also prophesied doom. She'd been given the gift of prophecy by Apollo, but when she rejected his romantic advances, he cursed her. She would always speak the truth, but no one would ever believe her.

She told them exactly what would happen. The horse was full of Greek warriors. They would emerge at night, and then Troy would burn. Everyone would die. She begged them not to bring it inside.

No one believed her. They never did. Some thought she was mad. Others found her prophecies annoying. Everyone dismissed her warnings.

The Trojans decided they would bring the horse inside. They tore down part of their own wall to fit the horse through the gates—the very walls that had protected them for ten years. They dragged the massive wooden horse into the city center. They crowned it with flowers. They celebrated their victory with feasts and wine, drinking late into the night.

While Troy slept, drunk and exhausted from celebrating, the horse's belly opened. Rope ladders dropped down. Odysseus, Menelaus, Diomedes, Neoptolemus, and the others climbed down silently.

They killed the guards at the gates and lit signal fires. The Greek army, which was waiting nearby, saw the fires and advanced. Thousands of Greek warriors poured into the undefended city.

The Sack of Troy

The Greeks showed no mercy. They'd lost friends, brothers, and sons. They'd been away from home for a decade. Achilles was dead. Ajax was dead, having fallen into a fit of madness and killing himself out of shame. Thousands of Greeks had died. Now they took revenge.

The slaughter was systematic and brutal. They killed every Trojan man they found. Age didn't matter—old men were cut down, young boys were murdered. Fighters died with weapons in their hands. Noncombatants were killed in their homes.

King Priam was murdered in his palace in one of the war's most horrific scenes. The elderly king took refuge, holding onto the altar, begging the gods for aid. In Greek culture, killing someone at an altar was among the most impious acts imaginable. Neoptolemus, Achilles's son, didn't care. He dragged Priam from the altar. Some versions say Neoptolemus first killed Priam's young son, Polites, in front of him. Then he butchered the king at the sacred stone, his blood soaking into it. Priam had lived to see his city destroyed and his sons killed, then died without dignity.

Astyanax, Hector's infant son, presented a problem. The Greeks knew that if any male heir survived, he might grow up to avenge Troy and rebuild the city. Different sources blame different people—some say Odysseus made the call, while others say Neoptolemus carried out the deed. Either way, someone took the baby from his mother's arms and threw him from Troy's high walls. The child's skull shattered on the rocks below. Andromache, his mother, was forced to watch.

Polyxena, one of Priam's daughters, was sacrificed on Achilles's tomb. Achilles's ghost had appeared demanding this honor, or Neoptolemus had decided his father deserved a grand funeral sacrifice. The young woman was dragged to the tomb and slaughtered like an animal. Her blood was poured over Achilles's grave.

Hecuba, Priam's wife and Troy's queen, lost everything. Her husband was murdered. Most of her sons were killed, including Hector, Paris, and Polites. Her daughters were taken as slaves. Her grandson was murdered. One son, Polydorus, had been sent away for safety before the war. When Hecuba learned he'd also been killed (betrayed by the host who was supposed to protect him), she went mad. In Euripides's play *Hecuba*, she transforms into a dog, either literally through divine punishment or metaphorically through her complete loss of humanity to grief and rage.

Andromache, Hector's widow, was claimed by Neoptolemus as his war prize. She would spend years as a slave before eventually being freed and remarrying.

Cassandra was claimed by Agamemnon. During the chaos of the sack, she'd taken refuge in Athena's temple, clinging to the goddess's statue for protection. Ajax the Lesser (son of Oileus) found her there and raped her at the altar, dragging her from the statue so violently that it fell. This sacrilege enraged Athena, which was one reason the goddess would later destroy much of the Greek fleet on their return voyage.

Aeneas, one of Troy's greatest warriors, managed to escape during the chaos. He gathered his father, Anchises (who was too old to walk), his young son, Ascanius, and a few followers. They fled the burning city. Aeneas's escape was either divine intervention—Aphrodite was his mother and protected him—or simple luck. He would wander for years before eventually reaching Italy, where his descendants would found Rome. The Romans later claimed Trojan ancestry through him, turning Troy's destruction into their own origin story.

Helen was returned to Menelaus. The sources disagree wildly on what happened, though. In some versions, Menelaus came to Troy's palace intent on killing her. She'd betrayed him, caused the war, and cost thousands of lives. He raised his sword. But then she let her robe fall. Her beauty stopped him cold. He couldn't kill her. He took her back to Sparta as his wife. In other versions, Greek soldiers wanted to stone her to death, but again, her beauty saved her. In still others, she'd never wanted to leave Sparta and was relieved to be rescued.

The city itself was destroyed. The Greeks looted the temples and palaces, taking gold, silver, bronze, and jewels—anything of value. Then they set fires. Troy burned through the night. The flames could be seen from far out at sea. The great city that had stood for generations was reduced to ash and rubble.

The level of brutality shocked even some Greeks. Murdering suppliants at altars, killing infants, and raping women in temples violated fundamental Greek values about honor in warfare. The gods were disgusted.

The burning of Troy by Johann Georg Trautmann.[36]

The Greeks would pay for their excessive cruelty. Most would never make it home.

The Price of Victory

Winning the war was one thing. Getting home was another. The Greeks' return journeys—collectively called the *nostoi* (returns)—were almost as disastrous as the war itself.

Agamemnon sailed home directly and reached Mycenae safely. He brought Cassandra, the Trojan prophetess, as his war prize. But his wife Clytemnestra had spent ten years planning revenge for Iphigenia's sacrifice. She'd taken a lover, Aegisthus. When Agamemnon arrived and stepped into his bath, Clytemnestra and Aegisthus murdered him, trapping him in a net and stabbing him repeatedly. Cassandra, who'd prophesied this and been ignored as always, was killed alongside him. Agamemnon survived the war only to be murdered in his own palace.

Menelaus got his wife back but faced years of wandering. Storms blew his fleet off course to Egypt and beyond. He and Helen traveled for seven years before finally reaching Sparta.

Diomedes returned to find his wife had taken a lover. Driven from his own kingdom, he eventually settled in Italy and founded several cities there.

Ajax the Lesser (son of Oileus, not the Ajax who killed himself) committed a terrible crime during Troy's sack. He dragged Cassandra from Athena's temple, where she'd sought sanctuary, and raped her at the goddess's altar. Athena was furious. On Ajax's voyage home, she had Poseidon shipwreck his fleet. Ajax survived and boasted that he'd escaped despite the gods' will. Poseidon, insulted, split the rock Ajax clung to with his trident, and Ajax drowned.

Neoptolemus, Achilles's son, was warned not to travel by sea. He went overland and eventually reached his homeland, but his brutal nature (he'd murdered Priam at an altar and possibly thrown the infant Astyanax from Troy's walls) meant he died violently himself in later years.

Odysseus faced the longest return of all. His journey took ten years—the same length as the war. He encountered the Cyclops Polyphemus, the witch Circe, the Sirens, the monsters Scylla and Charybdis, and the nymph Calypso, who held him captive for seven years. All his men died. His ship was destroyed. He returned alone to find his palace overrun with suitors trying to marry his wife, Penelope, and claim his throne. But that's a whole other story—one we will cover in the next chapter.

The Trojan War destroyed Troy, but it also broke the Greek army.
The few survivors limped home to changed kingdoms, dead families, or
usurped thrones. The age of heroes ended not in glory but in exhaustion.

Chapter 8: The Odyssey — Ten Years to Get Home

The Trojan War lasted ten years, according to Greek tradition. Odysseus's journey home took another ten.

Most of the Greek warriors who survived the siege of Troy either returned home within months or died trying. But Odysseus, king of Ithaca, faced obstacle after obstacle, monster after monster, and divine interference from a god who really knew how to hold a grudge.

Homer's *Odyssey* is the story of that journey. It is one of the greatest adventure tales ever told. It's about a clever man trying desperately to get back to his wife and son, facing impossible challenges with nothing but his wits and his determination to survive.

It's also about what happens at home when you're gone for twenty years. Odysseus's wife, Penelope, waited, besieged by suitors who wanted to marry her and claim Odysseus's throne. His son, Telemachus, grew up without a father. His kingdom slowly fell apart.

This is the story of how Odysseus finally made it home, whom he lost along the way, and what he found when he finally arrived.

The Journey Begins: Leaving Troy

When Troy fell, Odysseus was ready to go home. He'd been gone for ten years. He'd fought, and he'd helped design the Trojan Horse that ended the war. Now he just wanted to see his wife, Penelope, and his son, Telemachus, who'd been an infant when he left.

Odysseus commanded twelve ships with crews totaling around six hundred men from Ithaca and the surrounding islands. They loaded the ships with plunder from Troy and set sail.

The journey from Troy to Ithaca should have taken a few weeks at most. Instead, it took ten years. Almost immediately, things started going wrong.

The Cicones

Odysseus's first stop was the city of Ismarus, home of the Cicones. This was a raid, not an accident. The Cicones had been allies of Troy, and Odysseus wanted more plunder.

The raid succeeded. Odysseus's men sacked the city, killed the men, and took the women and treasure. Odysseus ordered his men to leave immediately before reinforcements arrived.

However, his men didn't listen. They'd found wine and wanted to celebrate. They held a feast on the beach, drinking and eating, refusing to leave despite Odysseus's warnings.

The Cicones sent for help. At dawn, a massive force attacked. Odysseus's men, hungover and unprepared, were slaughtered. Six men from each ship died—seventy-two men in total.

The survivors fled to their ships and sailed away, grieving their dead companions.

The Lotus-Eaters

A storm blew Odysseus's fleet off course to the land of the Lotus-Eaters. These people weren't hostile. They were friendly, peaceful, and happy to share their food.

The problem was the food itself. The lotus plant they ate made anyone who tasted it forget everything else. You stopped caring about home, family, duties, or the future. You just wanted to eat more lotus and drift in pleasant forgetfulness.

Odysseus sent three scouts to explore. The Lotus-Eaters gave them lotus to eat. The scouts forgot about their mission. They forgot about their ships and their home. They just sat there, content to do nothing forever.

Odysseus had to drag them back to the ships by force while they cried and struggled, desperate for more lotus. He tied them down below deck until the effects wore off, then quickly sailed away before anyone else could be tempted.

The Cyclops:
When Curiosity Almost Gets Everyone Killed

Odysseus's next stop became his most famous adventure—and his biggest mistake.

They reached an island inhabited by Cyclopes, giant one-eyed shepherds who lived in caves. They had no laws, grew no crops, and didn't even interact with each other except to occasionally steal sheep. Each Cyclops lived alone, answerable to no one.

Odysseus should have left immediately. But he was curious. He wanted to see these creatures and maybe get gifts from them (as was customary when strangers visited). He took twelve of his best men and went to explore, leaving the ships with the rest of the crew.

They found a cave filled with cheeses, milk pens full of lambs and kids, and all the supplies of a wealthy shepherd. Odysseus's men begged him to steal what they could and leave. Odysseus wanted to meet the cave's owner and see what gifts he'd offer.

This decision doomed them.

The Cyclops who owned the cave was Polyphemus, son of Poseidon. He was massive—twice the height of a normal man and the strength of ten men. He had a single eye in the middle of his forehead.

Polyphemus returned with his flocks, drove them into the cave, and sealed the entrance with a boulder so large that twenty teams of oxen couldn't budge it. Then he noticed the intruders.

Odysseus tried diplomacy. He explained they were Greek warriors returning from Troy, asked for hospitality (which was sacred to the gods), and requested gifts, as was traditional.

Polyphemus responded, "Cyclopes don't care about Zeus or the gods. We're stronger than they are."

Then he grabbed two of Odysseus's men, smashed their heads against the cave floor, and ate them raw. He washed them down with milk and went to sleep.

Odysseus considered killing Polyphemus as he slept, but he realized that the boulder sealed the cave entrance. If they killed Polyphemus, they'd be trapped forever. Only the Cyclops was strong enough to move that stone.

The next morning, Polyphemus ate two more men for breakfast, moved the boulder to let his flocks out, and then sealed it again, with Odysseus and his remaining men trapped inside.

Odysseus had to think fast. He found a massive wooden club in the cave (it was Polyphemus's walking stick). He and his men cut off a section, sharpened it into a stake, and hardened the point in the fire.

When Polyphemus returned that evening and ate two more men for dinner, Odysseus offered him strong, undiluted wine from their supplies.

Polyphemus had never tasted wine before. He loved it. He drank bowl after bowl. In his drunkenness, he became almost friendly. He asked Odysseus his name.

Odysseus answered, "My name is Nobody" (Outis in Greek).

Polyphemus, drunk and feeling generous, said, "Nobody, I'll eat you last. That's my gift to you." Then he passed out.

Odysseus and his men heated the wooden stake in the fire until it glowed red. Then, together, they drove it into Polyphemus's single eye, twisting and grinding it in. The eye boiled and popped. Polyphemus screamed in agony.

His neighbors, other Cyclopes from nearby caves, heard the screaming and came to his door. "Polyphemus, what's wrong? Who's attacking you?"

Polyphemus shouted, "Nobody is attacking me! Nobody is killing me!"

The other Cyclopes assumed that he was having a nightmare or was sick. "If no one's attacking you, then it must be divine punishment. Pray to your father Poseidon." They left.

The next morning, the blind Polyphemus opened the cave to let his flocks out, positioning himself at the entrance to feel each animal as it passed to make sure no men escaped. The sheep went out. The goats went out.

Odysseus had tied his men underneath the sheep—three sheep per man, with the man clinging to the belly of the middle sheep. When the sheep passed through, Polyphemus felt their backs and fleeces but didn't check underneath.

Odysseus himself clung to the belly of the largest ram. Polyphemus felt it and spoke sadly to his favorite ram. "Why are you last today? Usually you lead the flock. Are you grieving for your master's eye, blinded by Nobody and his wicked friends? If only you could speak and tell me where they're hiding!"

The ram passed through with Odysseus hidden beneath.

They made it to the ships and drove some of Polyphemus's sheep aboard as supplies. They started rowing away.

And then Odysseus made a fatal mistake. As they rowed away, Odysseus couldn't help himself. He shouted back at the cave, "Cyclops! If anyone asks who blinded you, tell them it was Odysseus, sacker of cities, son of Laertes, king of Ithaca!"

This was hubris in its truest Greek sense. This was not just pride, but a violent overstepping of boundaries, a refusal to show restraint even when restraint showed wisdom. Odysseus felt the need to claim credit for his cleverness, to make sure his name was attached to the victory. That need destroyed him.

Polyphemus roared with rage. He grabbed a mountain peak and hurled it at the voice. The rock landed just in front of Odysseus's ship, creating a wave that almost drove them back to shore. Odysseus's men rowed frantically, barely escaping.

Odysseus and Polyphemus *by Arnold Böcklin.*[27]

But the damage was done. Polyphemus now knew who had blinded him. He prayed to his father Poseidon, "Father, god of the sea, if I am truly your son, hear my prayer. Make Odysseus suffer. Let him lose all his companions. Let him reach home late, in a stranger's ship, broken, and let him find trouble in his house."

Poseidon heard. The god who controlled the seas now had a personal grudge against Odysseus.

One moment of pride turned the rest of Odysseus's journey into a nightmare.

Aeolus, the Laestrygonians, and Circe: Losing Almost Everything

The Bag of Winds

Odysseus's next stop brought hope. King Aeolus, keeper of the winds, hosted them for a month. When they left, Aeolus gave Odysseus an incredible gift: a leather bag containing all the storm winds. Only the West Wind was left free to blow them home.

For nine days, they sailed smoothly. Odysseus didn't sleep. He steered the ship himself, not trusting anyone else with such an important task. On the ninth day, they could see Ithaca. They were almost home. Odysseus, exhausted, finally fell asleep.

His men, curious and greedy, assumed the bag contained treasure that Odysseus was keeping for himself. While he slept, they opened it.

All the storm winds exploded out at once. A massive tempest blew the ships all the way back to Aeolus's island. Days of progress had been lost in minutes.

Odysseus begged Aeolus for help again, but Aeolus refused. "You must be cursed by the gods. I won't help someone the gods hate. Get off my island."

They sailed away, the winds now against them.

The Laestrygonians

They next reached the land of the Laestrygonians, another race of Giants, but these were far more dangerous than the Cyclopes.

Odysseus, cautious after Polyphemus, anchored his ship outside the harbor and sent scouts. The other eleven ships sailed straight into the harbor, which was surrounded by high cliffs.

The scouts found the Laestrygonians' city. These Giants weren't shepherds like Polyphemus. They were organized and had a king. But they were also cannibals who hunted humans like animals.

The king grabbed one scout and ate him. The other two ran. The Giants gathered at the harbor's entrance and began hurling boulders down from the cliffs, smashing the ships like a fisherman spearing fish in a barrel. Men fell into the water and were impaled on spears or eaten.

Odysseus, whose ship was outside the harbor, cut his anchor cable and ordered his men to row for their lives. They escaped.

Every other ship was destroyed. Of the six hundred men who'd left Troy, only Odysseus's crew of about fifty survived. In one afternoon, Odysseus lost 90 percent of his forces.

They sailed on, grieving and alone.

Circe the Witch

The survivors reached Aeaea, home of the goddess Circe. She was beautiful, powerful, and extremely dangerous.

Odysseus split his remaining men into two groups. One group, led by Eurylochus, went to explore. They found Circe's house surrounded by tame wolves and lions, some of whom were men she'd transformed with her magic.

Circe invited them inside for food and wine. Everyone entered except Eurylochus, who suspected a trap and hid. Circe drugged the wine. The moment the men drank, she struck them with her wand and transformed them into pigs. She locked them in pens and fed them acorns.

Eurylochus ran back and reported what had happened to Odysseus. Odysseus, despite having lost almost everything, prepared to face Circe alone.

The god Hermes appeared and gave him a magical herb called *moly* that would protect him from Circe's magic. Hermes also gave him advice: when Circe tries to transform him, he should draw his sword and make her swear by the gods not to harm him.

Odysseus followed the plan. He drank Circe's drugged wine. When she struck him with her wand, the *moly* protected him. He drew his sword. Circe, shocked that her magic had failed, realized this must be Odysseus, who had been prophesied to visit her island.

She swore by the gods not to harm him and turned his men back into humans. Then she became their host for an entire year.

The year on Aeaea was pleasant. Circe was generous. Food and wine were abundant. The men rested, recovering from their trauma. Odysseus and Circe even became lovers.

But eventually, Odysseus's men reminded him that they needed to go home.

Circe agreed to let them leave, but first, she gave Odysseus terrible news. Before he could return to Ithaca, he had to visit the underworld and consult the prophet Tiresias. He alone could tell Odysseus how to get home, what dangers still awaited him, and how to appease the gods he had angered, especially Poseidon.

Odysseus wept. No living person ever wanted to visit the land of the dead.

The Underworld, the Sirens, and Scylla: The Darkest Part of the Journey

The Land of the Dead

Following Circe's instructions, Odysseus sailed to the edge of the world, where the land of the living meets the land of the dead. There, he performed a ritual. He dug a pit, poured offerings of milk, honey, wine, and water, and then sacrificed sheep.

The blood flowed into the pit. The shades of the dead, drawn by the blood, came swarming, desperate to drink and temporarily regain consciousness and speech.

Odysseus held them back with his sword until Tiresias appeared. The prophet drank the blood and told Odysseus his future. He would reach home, but Poseidon was still angry. His journey would be hard. When he reached Ithaca, he'd find suitors in his house, trying to marry his wife and steal his kingdom. He'd have to kill them all.

Tiresias gave one critical warning. When he reached the island of Thrinacia, he would find the cattle of the sun god Helios. Tiresias told Odysseus that he must not harm those cattle. If he did, his ship would be destroyed, and all his men would die. Odysseus might survive, but he would arrive home alone.

After Tiresias, Odysseus spoke with other shades. His mother Anticlea appeared; he hadn't even known she'd died. She told him she died of grief, waiting for him to return. He tried three times to embrace her, but she was insubstantial, like mist.

Odysseus also spoke with Achilles, who delivered his famous line, "I'd rather be a slave on earth than king of all the dead." Even the greatest hero envied the living.

Ajax refused to speak to him. He was still angry that Odysseus had won Achilles's armor. Even in death, he couldn't forgive Odysseus for that wound to his honor.

Finally, Odysseus left, his ship filled with prophecies and grief.

The Sirens

Circe had warned Odysseus about the dangers ahead. First, he would encounter the Sirens.

The Sirens were creatures (part woman, part bird in most accounts) who sat on an island and sang. Their song was so beautiful, so irresistible, that any sailor who heard it would steer toward them, crash on the rocks, and die. The island was surrounded by rotting corpses and bones.

Circe's advice was to plug the men's ears with beeswax so they couldn't hear. If Odysseus wanted to hear the song, he should have his men tie him to the mast and order them not to release him, no matter what he said.

Odysseus did exactly this. As they approached, his men's ears were plugged, and he was tied to the mast.

The Sirens sang. Their song wasn't just beautiful; it was also seductive because of what it promised. They offered knowledge. They claimed to know everything that had happened at Troy, everything about Odysseus's struggles, everything worth knowing in the world. "Come to us, Odysseus, glory of Greece. We know all that happened in Troy. Listen and learn. No one leaves here unchanged."

The promise of complete knowledge, of understanding everything, was irresistible to him. Odysseus went mad with desire. He screamed at his men to untie him, to steer toward the voices. His men, ears plugged, couldn't hear him. Following his earlier orders, they tied him tighter.

The ship sailed past, and the song faded. Odysseus collapsed, exhausted from struggling.

He was the only person to hear the Sirens' song and survive.

Scylla and Charybdis

Next came an impossible choice. The ship had to pass through a narrow strait. On one side was Charybdis, a massive whirlpool that sucked down entire ships three times a day. On the other side was Scylla, a six-headed monster living in a cave high on a cliff.

Circe had warned him that he could not fight Scylla. She was immortal, a daughter of primordial gods. If he sailed too close to her, she would take six men—one per head. If he sailed close to Charybdis, she would destroy his entire ship. He could lose six men or everyone.

Odysseus hated this choice, but he had to make it.

He steered close to Scylla's cliff. He didn't tell his men about Scylla— what good would it do? They'd panic, and he couldn't prevent it anyway.

As they rowed past, Scylla struck. Six necks extended from the cave, six heads darted down, and six men were snatched from the deck. Odysseus heard them screaming his name as they were pulled up to the cave, still reaching toward him.

Those six men were the price of everyone else's survival. They'd passed the strait. They were still alive and almost home.

And then they reached Thrinacia, the island of the sun god's cattle.

The Final Disaster and Survival

The Cattle of the Sun

Odysseus remembered Tiresias's warning: do not harm the cattle of Helios. He told his men they would sail past Thrinacia without stopping.

But Eurylochus and the crew were exhausted. They'd been sailing and rowing for days. They begged to stop and rest on the island for just one night.

Odysseus agreed but made them swear an oath not to touch the cattle. They had plenty of food from Circe. They would just rest and then leave in the morning.

They swore. The men landed and set up camp.

The weather turned. Storm winds blew for a full month, keeping them stranded on the island. Their supplies ran out. They hunted game and fished, but it wasn't enough. They were slowly starving.

One day, while Odysseus was inland praying to the gods for help, Eurylochus convinced the men to slaughter some of Helios's cattle. Yes, the gods would be angry, but they were dying anyway. At least if they eat, they might survive. And if the gods destroyed them at sea, drowning would be quicker than starvation. Either way, they were dead. Might as well die with full stomachs.

The logic was terrible, but they were desperate. They killed several cattle and feasted.

The cattle were immortal. Even dead, their hides crawled, and their meat mooed on the spits. The gods knew immediately what had happened.

Helios went to Zeus. He told him, "Punish Odysseus's men for killing my cattle. If you don't, I'll go down to the underworld and shine among the dead instead of the living."

Zeus promised, "When they sail again, I'll destroy their ship with a thunderbolt."

When the winds finally changed, Odysseus returned to find his men had broken their oath. He knew they were doomed. But what choice did he have? Stay on the island and starve, or sail and face divine wrath?

They sailed.

Alone at Sea

As soon as they were out of sight of land, Zeus sent a storm. Black clouds gathered. The wind shrieked. Then a thunderbolt struck the ship directly.

The mast snapped, and the ship broke apart. Odysseus's men were thrown into the water and drowned. Odysseus only survived by lashing the mast and keel together into a makeshift raft. He clung to it as the storm blew him back toward Scylla and Charybdis.

Charybdis was just sucking down water when he arrived. His raft was pulled toward the whirlpool. Odysseus jumped and grabbed a fig tree growing from the cliff above Charybdis, where he hung for hours while his raft was sucked down into the whirlpool.

Eventually, Charybdis spat the wreckage back up. Odysseus dropped back into the water, grabbed the floating timbers, and paddled away with his hands, praying Scylla wouldn't attack again.

She didn't. He drifted for nine days, alone on the ocean, the only survivor of all the men who'd left Troy.

On the ninth day, he washed up on Ogygia, home of the nymph Calypso.

Seven Years with Calypso

Calypso was beautiful and lonely. She fell in love with Odysseus immediately. She offered him a home, a paradise island where he could live forever without pain, aging, or death. All he had to do was stay with her and forget about Ithaca.

Odysseus refused. He wanted to go home. He wanted to see his wife, his son, and his kingdom again. He wanted his life, even though it meant aging and eventually dying.

But Calypso wouldn't let him leave. She had no ship to offer him, and the island was too far from any shipping lane for him to signal passing ships. He was trapped.

Calypso by George Hitchcock.[38]

For seven years, Odysseus stayed on Ogygia. During the day, he sat on the beach and stared at the horizon, weeping. At night, Calypso compelled him to her bed. He was physically present but emotionally absent, trapped between gratitude for her saving his life and desperate longing for Ithaca.

Finally, Athena intervened. She went to Zeus and begged him to send Hermes to order Calypso to release Odysseus. Zeus agreed. Poseidon was away, so he couldn't object.

Hermes delivered the message. Calypso was bitter, but she had to obey Zeus. She helped Odysseus build a raft and gave him supplies.

After seven years, Odysseus finally sailed away from Ogygia. Poseidon returned and saw him. He sent one final storm. The raft was destroyed, and Odysseus almost drowned.

But with help from a sea goddess who took pity on him, Odysseus washed up on Scheria, land of the Phaeacians.

The Phaeacians

The Phaeacians were a blessed people. They were civilized, peaceful, skilled sailors, favored by the gods. Their princess, Nausicaa, found Odysseus naked and half dead on the beach.

She gave him clothes and directed him to her father's palace. King Alcinous welcomed the stranger, not yet knowing who he was.

At a feast that night, a blind poet sang songs about the Trojan War. Odysseus, listening, broke down and wept.

Alcinous stopped the song and asked, "Who are you? Why does this song make you weep?"

And Odysseus told his story. The Cyclops, Circe, the underworld, the Sirens, Scylla and Charybdis, the cattle of the sun, Calypso. The Phaeacians were amazed. They gave him gifts and promised to take him home in one of their magical ships. Their ships were so fast that they could cross any distance in a single day.

They loaded Odysseus aboard with treasure, and he fell asleep from exhaustion. When he woke, he was home. He was in Ithaca after twenty years away.

The Phaeacians had left him sleeping on the beach and sailed away. Poseidon, furious that they'd helped his enemy, turned their ship to stone as it returned to Scheria. The Phaeacians never helped travelers again.

But nevertheless, Odysseus was finally home.

Now came the hardest part: reclaiming his kingdom.

The Return: Reclaiming Ithaca

Odysseus woke on Ithaca, but he didn't recognize it. Athena had hidden the landmarks in mist. When he finally realized where he was, he should have been overjoyed. Instead, he was cautious.

Twenty years is a long time. He'd been declared dead. His kingdom might have been taken over. He needed information before revealing himself.

Athena appeared and told him the situation. His palace was overrun with suitors. Over one hundred men had come to court his wife, Penelope, claiming Odysseus was dead and demanding she choose a new husband. They'd been living in his house for years, eating his food, drinking his wine, abusing his servants, and trying to pressure Penelope into remarriage.

Penelope had been delaying them with a clever trick. She said she'd choose a husband when she finished weaving a funeral shroud for Odysseus's father, Laertes. Every day, she wove. Every night, she secretly unraveled what she'd woven. For three years, this worked. But eventually, a servant betrayed her, and the suitors forced her to finish the shroud.

Penelope and the Suitors by John William Waterhouse.[29]

Now she couldn't delay anymore. The suitors were getting violent, threatening her son, Telemachus, and demanding she choose.

Odysseus needed a plan. Athena disguised him as an old beggar, and he went to find his son.

Telemachus had been away searching for news of his father. Athena arranged for him to return home at just the right time to meet Odysseus at the hut of Eumaeus, Odysseus's loyal swineherd.

Athena temporarily lifted Odysseus's disguise. Father and son saw each other for the first time—Telemachus had been a baby when Odysseus left. Now he was a young man.

They embraced and wept. Then they planned.

Telemachus would return to the palace. Odysseus would follow, still disguised as a beggar. They would hide all the weapons in the hall. Then, when the time was right, they would kill all 108 suitors.

The Beggar in His Own House

Odysseus entered his palace dressed as a beggar. The suitors mocked him, threw food at him, and insulted him. He endured it all silently, watching and waiting.

His old dog, Argos, was lying on a dung heap. He had been neglected for twenty years, waiting for his master to return. When Odysseus approached, Argos recognized him. The dog wagged his tail and tried to approach, but he was too weak. Odysseus, still disguised, couldn't reveal himself. He walked past. Argos died, having seen his master one final time.

Penelope, hearing about the beggar, invited him to speak with her. He claimed to be a traveler who'd once met Odysseus. He described Odysseus accurately. Penelope wept, missing her husband.

The beggar told her, "I've heard Odysseus is alive and will return soon."

But Penelope didn't believe him. There had been too many false rumors over the years. Still, she was kind to the beggar, ordering her servants to wash his feet and give him a place to sleep.

His old nurse, Eurycleia, washed his feet. She noticed a scar on his leg—a scar that Odysseus had received from a boar hunt in his youth. She looked up at him in recognition.

Odysseus grabbed her throat and whispered, "Don't tell anyone. Not even Penelope. Not yet."

Eurycleia swore silence.

The Contest

The next day, Penelope announced a contest. Whoever could string Odysseus's massive bow and shoot an arrow through twelve ax heads in a row would become her husband.

None of the suitors could even string the bow. It was too strong, as it was designed specifically for Odysseus's strength.

The beggar asked to try. The suitors mocked him, but Penelope allowed it.

Odysseus took the bow. He examined it like an old friend. Then, effortlessly, he strung it. He tested it, and it sang like a harp string. He took an arrow, drew, and fired. The arrow passed cleanly through all twelve ax heads.

The suitors realized something was wrong. But it was too late.

Odysseus threw off his disguise. Telemachus brought out weapons. Odysseus's first arrow killed the leader of the suitors, Antinous, striking him in the throat as he drank wine.

The suitors panicked. They tried to grab weapons, but Telemachus had hidden them all. They were trapped in the hall, unarmed, facing Odysseus with a quiver of arrows and righteous rage.

Odysseus shot them all down. When the arrows ran out, he and Telemachus fought with spears and swords. Some suitors begged for mercy. Odysseus gave none. They'd abused his household, threatened his son, harassed his wife, and consumed his wealth for years.

All 108 suitors died. The servants who'd been disloyal died with them. The hall ran with blood.

The Reunion

Penelope didn't believe it at first. After twenty years of false hopes and rumors, she couldn't trust that Odysseus had really returned.

So, she tested him. She told a servant to move their marriage bed out of their bedroom. Odysseus exploded, "That's impossible! I built that bed myself, carved it from a living olive tree still rooted in the ground. One post is the tree itself. Unless someone sawed through the trunk, that bed cannot be moved."

Only Odysseus knew this secret. Penelope finally believed it was really him. She ran to her husband, and they embraced. At last, they were reunited.

But the story doesn't quite end there. Odysseus still had to deal with the families of the dead suitors, all of whom wanted revenge. More blood would have been spilled if Athena hadn't intervened.

As Odysseus and his allies prepared to face them, Athena appeared among the ranks of the angry men. She raised her staff and cast a veil of calm over everyone, urging them to lay down their weapons and stop the cycle of bloodshed. She reminded them that the slaughter of the suitors was fated and just and that further violence would only bring more grief and suffering.

The warriors laid aside their spears and swords. Peace was restored.

Odysseus's journey was over. It had cost him nearly everything, but the *Odyssey* ends with Odysseus and Penelope together, telling each other their stories late into the night.

After twenty years apart, they were together again.

Conclusion
Why These Stories Still Matter

You made it! From the creation of the cosmos to Odysseus finally getting home, you've traveled through the major myths of ancient Greece.

But here's the real question: why does any of this matter? These stories are thousands of years old. The Greeks who told them are dust. The gods they worshiped don't exist. Troy is a pile of ruins. The heroes never actually lived. So why are we still talking about them?

Because these stories are still true.

Not literally—there was no Zeus throwing thunderbolts, no Medusa with snake hair, no Minotaur in a labyrinth. But the stories capture something true about human nature, about power and pride, about love and loss, and about the patterns that repeat across every culture and every century.

Greek mythology endures because it presents human experience without promising an easy resolution or cosmic justice. Modern culture loves to promise that everything will work out. Work hard, and you'll succeed. Be good, and you'll be rewarded. The universe has a plan. Everything happens for a reason.

Greek mythology presents suffering without promising a happy ending. Ancient Greece believed in fate. A plan existed, but it didn't care whether you were good or bad. The Fates spun your thread, measured it, and cut it according to patterns mortals couldn't understand or change. This wasn't randomness; it was cosmic order that operated independently of human morality or desire.

This honesty is brutal but valuable. Rather than pretend the world was fair, the Greeks created myths that reflected reality as they experienced it. Life was full of war, disease, injustice, and random suffering.

Achilles was the greatest warrior who ever lived, and he died young from an arrow to the heel. Hector was noble and brave, and he died defending his brother's stupid mistake. Odysseus was clever enough to outsmart the Cyclops, but he still lost all his men. Orpheus did everything right to bring Eurydice back from death, but he failed at the last moment because he was human.

And yet—and this is crucial—the heroes still acted anyway.

Prometheus gave fire to humanity even though he knew he would be tortured forever. Achilles chose glory over a long life. Hector faced Achilles despite knowing he would lose.

They acted with courage, purpose, and meaning, not because the universe promises reward but because that's what it means to be human. You create your own meaning in a meaningless cosmos. You matter because you choose to matter.

That's a more profound heroism than fighting monsters who are destined to lose to you.

Here's another book by Matt Clayton that you might like

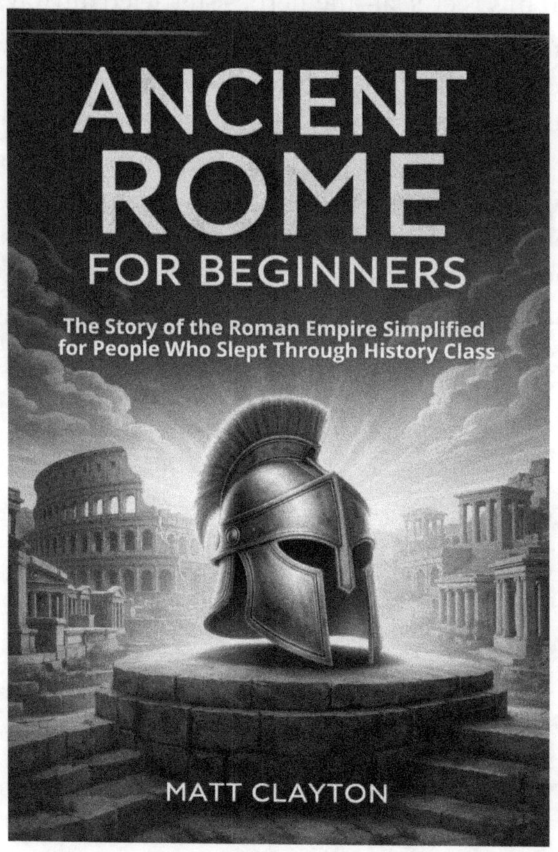

Free Bonus from Captivating History (Available for a Limited time)

Hi History Lovers!

Now you have a chance to join our exclusive history list so you can get your first history ebook for free as well as discounts and a potential to get more history books for free!

Simply visit the link below to join.

Or, Scan the QR code!

captivatinghistory.com/ebook

Also, make sure to follow us on Facebook, X, and YouTube by searching for Captivating History.

Sources

Buxton, Richard. *The Complete World of Greek Mythology.* London: Thames & Hudson, 2004.

Euripides. *Medea.* Translated by Rex Warner. In *Euripides I.* Chicago: University of Chicago Press, 1955.

Gantz, Timothy. *Early Greek Myth: A Guide to Literary and Artistic Sources.* Baltimore: Johns Hopkins University Press, 1993.

Hard, Robin. *The Routledge Handbook of Greek Mythology.* London: Routledge, 2004.

Hesiod. *Theogony.* Translated by M. L. West. Oxford: Oxford University Press, 1988.

Hesiod. *Works and Days.* Translated by M. L. West. Oxford: Oxford University Press, 1988.

Homer. *The Iliad.* Translated by Robert Fagles. New York: Penguin Classics, 1991.

Homer. *The Odyssey.* Translated by Robert Fagles. New York: Penguin Classics, 1996.

Morford, Mark P. O., Robert J. Lenardon, and Michael Sham. *Classical Mythology.* 10th ed. Oxford: Oxford University Press, 2013.

Ovid. *Metamorphoses.* Translated by A. D. Melville. Oxford: Oxford University Press, 1986.

Plutarch. *Life of Theseus.* Translated by Bernadotte Perrin. Cambridge, MA: Harvard University Press, 1914.

Virgil. *The Aeneid.* Translated by Robert Fagles. New York: Penguin Classics, 2006.

Image Sources

1 https://commons.wikimedia.org/wiki/File:Sandro_Botticelli_-
  _La_nascita_di_Venere_-_Google_Art_Project_-_edited.jpg

2 https://commons.wikimedia.org/wiki/File:Rubens_saturn.jpg

3 https://commons.wikimedia.org/wiki/File:Jupiter_Smyrna_Louvre_Ma13.jpg

4 https://commons.wikimedia.org/wiki/File:Leda_-_after_Michelangelo_Buonarroti.jpg

5 Luis García, CC BY-SA 3.0 <https://creativecommons.org/licenses/by-sa/3.0>, via
  Wikimedia Commons, https://commons.wikimedia.org/wiki/File:
  Neptuno_colosal_(Museo_del_Prado)_01.jpg

6 British Museum, CC BY 2.5 <https://creativecommons.org/licenses/by/2.5>, via
  Wikimedia Commons, https://commons.wikimedia.org/wiki/File:
  Persephone_Hades_BM_Vase_E82.jpg

7 National Roman Museum of the Altemps Palace, CC BY 2.5
  <https://creativecommons.org/licenses/by/2.5>, via Wikimedia Commons,
  https://commons.wikimedia.org/wiki/File:Demeter_Altemps_Inv8546.jpg

8 https://commons.wikimedia.org/wiki/File:Mattei_Athena_Louvre_Ma530_n2.jpg

9 https://commons.wikimedia.org/wiki/File:Vulcan_Coustou_Louvre_MR1814.jpg

10 https://commons.wikimedia.org/wiki/File:Dionysos_satyr_Altemps_Inv8606.jpg

11 https://commons.wikimedia.org/wiki/File:La_tortura_de_Prometeo,_por_
  Salvator_Rosa.jpg

12 Naples National Archaeological Museum, CC BY 2.5
  <https://creativecommons.org/licenses/by/2.5>, via Wikimedia Commons,
  https://commons.wikimedia.org/wiki/File:Herakles_Farnese_MAN_Napoli_Inv6001
  _n01.jpg

13 Carole Raddato from FRANKFURT, Germany, CC BY-SA 2.0 <https://creativecommons.org/licenses/by-sa/2.0>, via Wikimedia Commons, https://commons.wikimedia.org/wiki/File:Mosaic_with_the_Labors_of_Hercules,_3rd_century_AD,_found_in_Lliria_(Valencia),_National_Archaeological_Museum_of_Spain,_Madrid_(15457108142).jpg

14 https://commons.wikimedia.org/wiki/File:Perseo_y_Andr%C3%B3meda,_por_Tiziano.jpg

15 Aison, CC BY 2.5 <https://creativecommons.org/licenses/by/2.5>, via Wikimedia Commons, https://commons.wikimedia.org/wiki/File:Kylix_Theseus_Aison_MNA_Inv11365_n1.jpg

16 https://commons.wikimedia.org/wiki/File:Jason_and_Medea_-_John_William_Waterhouse.jpg

17 https://commons.wikimedia.org/wiki/File:Jas%C3%A3o_e_o_Velo_de_ouro_-_Bertel_Thorvaldsen_-_1803.jpg

18 https://commons.wikimedia.org/wiki/File:Psyche_et_LAmour.jpg

19 https://commons.wikimedia.org/wiki/File:Herbert_Draper_-_The_Lament_for_Icarus_-_Google_Art_Project.jpg)

20 https://commons.wikimedia.org/wiki/File:Charles_Fran%C3%A7ois_Jalabert_-_Nymphs_Listening_to_the_Songs_of_Orpheus_-_Walters_3737.jpg

21 https://commons.wikimedia.org/wiki/File:Punishment_sisyph.jpg

22 https://commons.wikimedia.org/wiki/File:Enrique_Simonet_-_El_Juicio_de_Paris_-_1904.jpg

23 https://commons.wikimedia.org/wiki/File:Charles_de_La_Fosse_-_Le_sacrifice_d%27Iphig%C3%A9nie_-_Google_Art_Project.jpg

24 https://commons.wikimedia.org/wiki/File:Peter_Paul_Rubens_181.jpg

25 Eugene Romanenko, CC BY 2.0 <https://creativecommons.org/licenses/by/2.0>, via Wikimedia Commons, https://commons.wikimedia.org/wiki/File:The_Triumph_of_Achilles_by_Franz_von_Matsch.jpg

26 https://commons.wikimedia.org/wiki/File:J_G_Trautmann_Das_brennende_Troja.jpg

27 https://commons.wikimedia.org/wiki/File:Arnold_B%C3%B6cklin_-_Odysseus_and_Polyphemus.jpg)

28 https://commons.wikimedia.org/wiki/File:Hitchcock,_George_-_Calypso_-_Google_Art_Project.jpg

29 https://commons.wikimedia.org/wiki/File:Penelope_and_the_Suitors_-_John_William_Waterhouse_-_ABDAG003035.jpg